THE NEW WEALTH

Magnetize Abundance
Hold Your Wealth
And Leave A Legacy

KERI NORLEY

First published in 2020 by Keri Norley
Colorado, USA
© Keri Norley

The moral rights of the author have been asserted.
This book is a SpiritCast Network Book.

Author:
    Norley, Keri
Title:
    The New Wealth; Magnetize Abundance, Hold Your Wealth, And Leave A Legacy
ISBN:
    978-1-716-48834-4

All rights reserved. No part of this book may be reproduced, stored in a retrieval system, communicated or transmitted in any form or by any means without prior written permission. All enquiries should be made to the publisher at keri@kerinorley.com

Editor-in-chief: Cherise Lily Nana
Cover Design: Sarah Rose Design

Disclaimer: The material in this publication is of the nature of general comment only, and does not represent professional advice. It is not intended to provide specific guidance for particular circumstances and it should not be relied on as the basis for any decision to take action or not take action on any matter which it covers. Readers should obtain professional advice where appropriate, before making any such decision. To the maximum extent permitted by law, the author and publisher disclaim all responsibility and liability to any person, arising directly or indirectly from any person taking or not taking action based on the information in this publication.

TABLE OF CONTENTS

Foreword V

Thank You Xiii

Section 1 Introduction 1

Section 2 The New Wealth Foundations 17

Section 3 An Overview Of Our Current Financial System 27

Section 4 What Does It Mean To Magnetize Abundance? 51

Section 5 Holding Your Wealth 87

Section 6 Leave Your Legacy 117

Section 7 The Currency In The New Wealth 141

Section 8 Bonus: What Do You Do When Your Partner Isn't Wanting Anything To Do With This Work? 161

Section 9 Welcome To 'The New Wealth' 167

Moving Forward In 'The New Wealth' 173

Testimonials For The New Wealth 186

FOREWORD

Keri, thank you for writing this book for humanity.
Thank you for being who you are.
Thank you for showing up in the world and saying yes to your soul, saying yes to your vision, saying yes to your highest self.
Thank you for being that for humanity, for being an example that no matter what, you can still show up.

I know your story. I know your anxiety attacks. I know the disorders you have had in your world which went deeper, deep, deeper than people can even think of.

No matter how many limitations you have had, how many patterns, how many ways you could have gotten distracted here and there, you always come back. You always say yes, you always go deeper, you always surrender more and more.

I'm so grateful that you are saying yes constantly to your highest self, and that you were so open to receive all this information and share it with the world. Thank you for doing this.

Thank you.

These are times where we need this information.

Knowledge is power.

Just by knowing, by remembering who we are and why we are here and by knowing what moment in time we are going through in this planetary alignment is so important right now.

THE NEW WEALTH

It is so important to let ourselves be touched and transformed by the energies that are being received right now in the planet more than ever. We are being gifted with very high frequencies that are available to us right now.

During these times, we get to choose to be grounded, to be focused, to be centered, to be in our bodies and accept what our current reality is.

It is a choice to be raw and real with ourselves so we can upgrade to the next level, so that we can be open to really receive the next level of our manifestation, the next level of the frequency that is waiting for us to open up so we can embody it.

This is a book for that. It not only gives you knowledge, but gives you the tools to be raw and real with yourself, with your life, so that you can say yes to the next level.

This book also gives you tools to transform, to do the transmutation, the alchemy from the core, from the nervous system.

One of the gifts for rewiring yourself is Quantum Flow. It takes you right into the nervous system so that you can shift and transform the body memory that has you stuck.

With Quantum Flow, you can transform stagnant energy into the energy of manifestation. It becomes the battery of your soul, the battery of manifestation.

We learn how to use the electric frequencies of the thoughts and the magnetic frequencies of the emotions in order to expand our field from our core. That's why it's so important to reconnect our core with our emotions, with our thoughts, with every muscle in our bodies.

Keri Norley

It is time in the world to stand up in every way we can, and that means wake up every layer of our being, everything we have available. It doesn't work anymore just to have 10%, 20% of what's available for us working for us. It won't work anymore because the rest that is underneath the surface is going to come up to be seen and dealt with in these turbulent times.

When we acknowledge and we are aware of our core and we are aware that there is so much stuck energy that can be transmuted and transcended through the spine all the way up into the brain, we can open up to our inner genius using the power of our core, using our gifts that are hidden, that are there behind the veil of illusion.

We remove the veil, we do the work, we do the alchemy, we reconnect to our core. We set our core for success, and then whatever comes into our life, whatever action comes from within, we move in life from that inner alignment.

Strategy is really just 20% of our success. 80% comes from inner alignment and that inner alignment comes from our core. Once we acknowledge who we are, our natural gifts, and why we are here, we can embody our gifts.

Once we have surrendered to our gifts and ignited them, we awaken them. Now we are ready to share them with the world.

It is our responsibility to show up and share these gifts with the world.
It is our birthright.
It is part of our sovereign being.

The abundance that we're craving goes beyond the material.

Abundance. What's behind abundance is really freedom.

THE NEW WEALTH

The freedom to feel alive and awake, to feel the authenticity and the uniqueness of who we really are that comes from within. And that needs to be shared with the world. It is here in our DNA to be awakened and shared with the world.

It is part of abundance. If we don't share, we will never feel that depth of abundance, that wholeness, where we don't feel anything or anyone from the outside because we have remembered who we are.

We have remembered that we are whole, that we are complete. And anything we call in comes from a place of abundance, not from scarcity, not from a place of need.

We don't 'need' anything.

And that's why I radiate my light out into the world and I share my gifts and I serve.
I accept that I am here to serve.

Every human being is here to serve on this planet.

The more I serve, the more I shine my light, the more I awaken my energy, the more I remember who I am, the more I can start flowing in my life. The more I have available to flow, the more tapped in I can be to the synchronicities of life, the more I can align.

If I'm in a high frequency and I awaken all those inner codes, I will be matching the codes that are available for me out there because of that inner awakening I just had.

Because of that high frequency, I will be emitting that signal out into the world in order to attract from my highest self, the highest gifts available for me right now to support my purpose in life.

In doing so, I receive the highest vibrational people, tribe, community relationships, the highest vibrational opportunities, the highest vibrational energy seen as money, or the energy of love, and/or of manifestation. This is available for all of us.

The high vibration is energy you can feel in your body. The highest vibration of thoughts, the highest vibrational emotions in every cell of our being allows us to awaken our connection to the divine.

We remember who we are, and that's where we align with our highest self. And life becomes full of ease, grace and flow.

We can use obstacles as opportunities. We learn to listen, to trust and to act from within knowing that we are guided, knowing that it goes beyond us, knowing that it's not about our personal reality, it's about that universal reality. And the more we tap into what the universal reality, the more we flow.

It is time to walk our talk.

This is reflected on how we walk in life, how we breathe, how we move, our posture, our thoughts, our emotions. We can't just be talking anymore and reciting theory as if we are books.

We are living sacred geometry, living vibrations, frequencies that are alive, pulsating and in order for us to keep that state of flow, we need to keep those frequencies in the highest possible.

Every time we have an expansion, every time we have a transmutation, every time we let go of an old pattern and we turn it into light, we bring the shadow back to the light. We then let it be integrated in every cell of our being, remembering who we are, always taking the time to go within and accept the energy, take it in into our bones, into our bone marrow, into our nervous system just to remember that that is our natural state.

We are here to receive, that the universe is gifting us all the time but we need to stop.
It's important to stop so we can listen.

Part of the process is the integration where we stop and we receive, and we say thank you.

Thank you life.

Thank you love.

Thank you light.

Thank you to myself for being open and receptive and surrendering to the process.

Thank you to the divine for guiding me and showing me that it's always been inside.

And the more we surrender to this, the more we tap into our divine truth, into our unlimited being, into our magnificence, into our full expansion that comes from within, not from a place of need but from a place of being, not from a place of doing, but from a place of being. The more we flow.

I am. I am. I am.

The more we tap into the I am, the more we are contributing to humanity.

The real contribution is about us saying yes to our full potential. It's about all of us committing to our own paths. And from there everything is going to flow, from there we can embody in every cell of our beings, Divine Truth.

This is who we are.
This is why we are here.

Thank you Keri for reminding us that everything is related and that now is the most important time to wake up our gifts and say yes to our full potential.

Thank you Keri for being an example for your family, for your community, for humanity that it is possible to transform the darkest shadows into light, that it is possible to take our lives to the next level.

Thank you for showing us that it is possible to say yes to our soul.

Thank you for sharing this gift with humanity.

I send you all my love.

I wish everyone the best journey.

I invite you all to open beyond your ears, feel the vibration, feel the frequencies that come through this book. It's way beyond words, it's way beyond philosophy.

It is experience, it is wisdom that has been shared so we can embody it and take our life to the next level.

With Love,

Juan Pablo Barahona

THE NEW WEALTH

PS- Keri has given you a gift in this book to be able to experience Quantum Flow.

You can access it at www.kerinorley.com/resources

Please make sure to do the flow and welcome yourself to the Quantum Flow familia.

Juan Pablo Barahona (JuanPa) is a Transformational Leader, Speaker, Serial Entrepreneur, Energy Master and Coach.

He is the founder of Juanpa Global and the Conscious Living School, two companies dedicated to awaken humanities full potential in every area of their life. He is the creator of The Quantum Flow Method, an embodiment technology that accelerates manifestation in the fastest way possible and brings humanity back to its natural state.

JuanPa can be seen in the movie Thrive 2. The Thrive movies are about Quantum Science and high vibrational living. If you haven't seen the Thrive movies watch them ASAP and check out their community.

JuanPa is featured on MindValley.

Author of The Abundance Codes.

As seen on ABC, Forbes, CBS, FOX, NBC, The Huffington Post, Inc, Entrepreneur

JuanPa is the real deal. He is a man of integrity and love.

Please go and follow him and his work. It will change your life, if you embrace this work.

THANK YOU

Ron Ben-Joseph

Without you, this book would not be what it is today. Thank you for being with me every step of the way. Thank you for helping me find this content for The New Wealth within me and finding ways to share it with the world.

Thank you for seeing me so fully, loving me so much and helping me step into being the messenger that I am today. I am infinitely grateful for you in my life.

Dave Thompson, Davina Davidson, and Nicole Lee Ann McLellan.

Thank you for your guidance, love and support for this book – this movement – to come to life. Thank you for always believing in me. Thank you for keeping me on track and never letting me give up. Thank you for seeing in me what I couldn't see in myself.

The book writing and publishing process was such a held process with you at the helm, Dave Thompson. Your knowledge and integrity in taking me through the whole process – from not knowing what I would be writing about, just knowing it was time, to becoming an Amazon Best Seller – is absolutely amazing. I'm so grateful to you all for being a part of this journey.

THE NEW WEALTH

Nikhil Kale

Thank you for taking what is in my heart and the field and bringing that into a visual representation of 'The New Wealth'.

The sigil for 'The New Wealth' was created by this amazing man along with the other aspects of bringing a multi-dimensional brand to life.

You are amazing and your poetic way of speaking melts my soul. I am so grateful for your help in tapping into the energy around this book, this movement and helping me bring it to life.

Pauline Martin-Brooks

My best friend in the world. Thank you for everything. There are no words necessary, because I know you know. And still, thank you.

You have been with me each step of the way in life and as I birth this book. You have given me things to think about to expand this message. You have invited me to show up as the best version of myself and I love you for all that you are.

I am grateful to have you in my life and have you walk alongside me. It's time to wake up the world, beautiful.

To my soul brothers and sisters that have been by my side supporting each other all along the way. Thank you.

Thank you to my Quantum Healing Family, Quantum Flow familia, Spiral Crew, local Denver friends, Mastermind sister, global friends, clients and family.

Thank you for being in my life. I am so grateful for all of you, amazing beings that are surrounding me. #togetherwerise

Keri Norley

Braincode Centers (Neurofeedback)

Thank you to the beautiful ladies, Angie, Erin, and Monica at Braincode Centers, who have been helping me with Neurofeedback.

Re-wiring my brain has been a critical part of being able to move forward in my life and bring this book into reality. Plus, thank you for your continual love and support as I have walked this road that has challenged me immensely to BE the person who brings this work to the world.

To my mentors

Leah Steele

Thank you for being a leader in the wealth consciousness space. Thank you for being one of my greatest mentors.

Regan Hillyer and Juan Pablo Barahona

The day that Quantum Healing Certification turned up in my field changed my life forever. I had NO IDEA what anything you were talking about meant, I just knew I had to be in Costa Rica with you and you felt it too. What a ride ever since.

Thank you for being two of the most beautiful beings to walk this planet in your integrity. I respect and love you both so much.

JuanPa, thank you for Quantum Flow. You have been a guiding light for me through some rough times on this planet and in my life and I am beyond grateful for your love and for this method to help me be in Flow. Thank you for never giving up on me and always seeing me in my highest and best.

THE NEW WEALTH

So many days over this year you have been in my ears, in my head, in my field helping me love myself through my pain and showing me that whatever has happened on my journey has happened, but that doesn't have to hold me back moving forward.

We get to shift our fields from the inside out. We truly get to live a life of Bliss, Abundance, Love, Joy and Peace. You show me this every day and I so deeply love you, brother.

It's an honour to be bringing Quantum Flow to the world with you and to activate the planet with this amazing way of life and movement.

Kate O'Brien

Your way of showing up in the world has asked me to play a different game.

Thank you for being such an inspiration.

Thank you for helping me create the website to support this book and movement.

Jessica Caver Lindholm

Thank you for being this gorgeous woman who exudes love and pleasure in life. You remind me every day what life can be and more. I am so grateful for yours and Luke Lindholm's presence in my life.

Thank you for constantly reminding me that I don't have to have accomplished everything before I even start. Thank you for giving me permission to be myself and be rewarded abundantly for it, and seeing the need for my work and encouraging me every step of the way.

Keri Norley

Vanessa Sumner

You are there for me when I need it most. You have helped me stretch and grow, seen me at my most vulnerable, and have loved, supported and helped me through so much. You help me come back home to the truth of who I am. You are magical and multi-dimensional, and I love how you stick to your own lane. You inspire me all the time.

Thank you for our conversations, for your amazing healing work, for sharing Andara crystals with the world and for your friendship and support. I am so grateful to be walking this path with you by my side.

Mom, Dad, and Marty

Thank you for your support over all of the years. Thank you for being there for me. Thank you for loving me, no matter what I throw your way. I obviously would not be who I am today without you in my life. I love you!

Hugh, Robbie and Sam. You three have been there for every joyous and pain-staking moment that I have been through to be in the place to bring this book – this movement – to life.

You have given up time to be with me. You have seen me work so much to be where I am now.

Thank you. From my heart to yours for all of your love and support as I walk my path. Thank you for your support in my crazy and wild ideas and for all the times you have come along for the ride.

I love you!

THE NEW WEALTH

Gram and gramps

This book would not be here if it wasn't for you. There is much written about you in this book so for now, I'll just say that you two are my guiding light and my biggest inspiration. I'm infinitely grateful to have had you as role models. I love you beyond all time and space.

To all of you

Thank you to all of you that are here reading this book. I'm excited for you that you have been called to this book and you have taken action and actually opened up this book.

When you turn (or click) the pages of this book, you are being activated into 'The New Wealth'.

This is for you. This is for me. This is for humanity.

#togetherwerise

SECTION 1
INTRODUCTION

Before we get stuck into the meat of this book, I'm going to share a little bit about my story and why this book is so important to me and the consciousness of the world.

I had the absolute privilege to grow up in a wealthy, successful family. I grew up living in the 1% within the 1%.

My grandfather owned the largest Chevrolet dealer in the United States for many years. He sold 1 million cars between the years of 1936-1986 and millions more after that.

In that time, he also went on to create "Fleet Car Leasing" as we know it, a way for companies to easily service their staff with cars and have someone else hold the responsibility and titles of the cars. That company has grown to be a multi-billion-dollar company that still has its original clients many decades later.

He didn't stop there. My grandfather had multiple investments and businesses along the way. He and my grandmother truly created a Business Empire.

If you have lived in Chicago, until the 2008 financial crash, you would have to be blind to have not known of my family. 'Z' Frank Chevrolet was an icon in Chicago.

THE NEW WEALTH

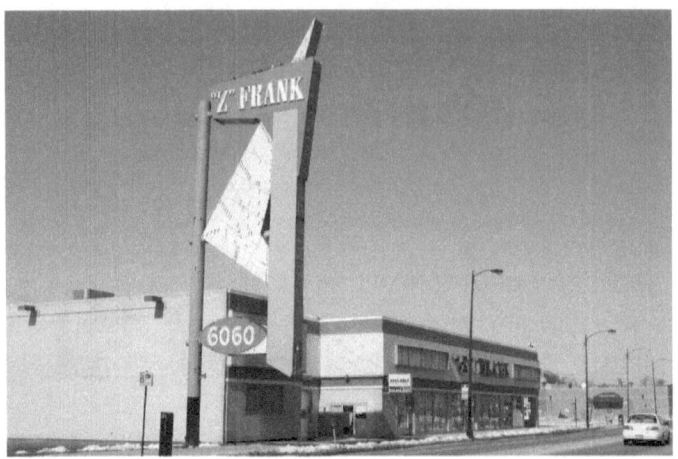

This sign, along with the dealership that went on for blocks, was an iconic sign in Chicago for many decades.

I grew up doing philanthropic work regularly. From choosing to spend my time helping kids with special needs, to galivanting around Chicago with my mom to help in her philanthropic endeavors, licking thousands of stamps and envelopes (before they could just be stuck together), going to fund-raising parties, dressing up for gala events, sitting at tables with multi-millionaires, and more, was a big part of my childhood. When doing school fund-raisers for anything… I would always raise the most money.

We belonged to a country club, where I would spend weekends and any spare minutes of my summer when I wasn't at day camp or overnight camp.

Family get-togethers for all holidays, with at least 50-people sit-down dinners at my grandparent's house with wait staff, was totally normal. Their home was an entertainer's dream and built so that they could do so. All extended family were invited, and no one was ever left out.

We couldn't wear jeans, casual or leisure attire at my grandparent's house. I had nice clothes to wear there and to the country club.

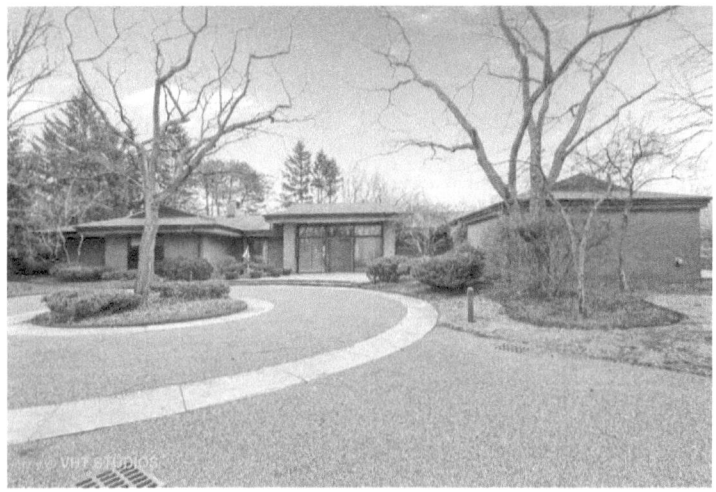

My grandparent's home

We were drilled in 'Miss Manners' and the appropriate way to 'behave'. Etiquette became second nature in dealing with my family, friends and business associates.

We travelled the world together. Family trips to Acapulco, Mexico and Sun Valley, Idaho for fishing in the summer were regulars for all 13 grandkids, 8 kids and my grandparents. We would often spend spring breaks in Palm Springs, California at my grandparent's house. If enough of us were there, we would have sleeping bags rolled out on the hallway floors. Again... Everyone got to be together and we all loved hanging out with each other.

With my personal passion for international travel and learning about new cultures and expanding my horizons, I had been on 6 continents of the world by the time I was 22.

THE NEW WEALTH

When I was in high school, my family had moved to a home on the north shore of Chicago that was huge. We had 7 bedrooms and the big hallway upstairs felt like a hotel. My mom even gave each room a name with a wooden placard over each door. We had an indoor pool, sauna and basement equipped with a pool table. It was a paradise for me and my friends.

I could go on and on about the life I was raised in, but I think you are getting my point by now. I'm saying this because when I talk about wealth, when I talk about money, when I talk about leaving a legacy, it's how I was raised.

I'm sharing this because I want to invite you into the world of wealth from an insider's perspective so that I can help you to let go of the stories that are in your head around money and wealth that are likely not true.

To truly be an Empress/Emperor or Queen/King, to live in a state of wealth, it's a training. It's a way of BEing in the world. It's a living, breathing experience of life.

My grandparents and family's influence around Chicago and the world touched millions and millions of people's lives; not only their business, but also their philanthropic work.

My grandmother was a part of starting initiatives that are still run today.

They have given Jewish kids the opportunity to have a place to come together and connect at summer camps.

They have spent millions of dollars to support hospitals and medical research and so much more.

I am so proud to be a part of this legacy.

I'm not sharing any of this to brag. Truthfully, I would have kept it behind closed doors for a lot longer, if it was for me.

I say this because I know what is available for us when we allow ourselves to receive true abundance. I know what philanthropic work we can do when we have the money to support it. I know how amazing it is to be able to live this abundant way of life and if this way of life calls you... if you desire to grow your wealth... I wish this for you, too.

That said, like anything in life, it comes with its own stuff too.

Living in this world, the expectations are high to succeed and perform and show up a certain way, marry a certain type of person, do a certain type of work... it can be stifling and hard to live up to.

In 2002, I left the US when I was 23 years young to live in Australia for the second time. I was studying a Diploma of Integrated Body Therapies in Sydney. I dove into all things natural health, bodywork, nutrition, energy, crystals and more. It was the opening of gates to a different way of living.

I got my residency through Skilled Migration for my Early Childhood Education Degree within about 9 months of moving to Australia. I knew it was home for me for a while.

I didn't realize it at the time, but inherently knew that I needed the space to be able to find my own way in the world. It was not easy, but it was my path. I married a gorgeous Aussie man and had my two beautiful sons, whilst living in Australia for nearly 15 years.

I have been obsessively studying, teaching, and supporting others to shift their mindset, energy, and physical world ever since. I help people create life as a spiritual practice and clear their fields of any of their blocks on an energetic, emotional, mental, physical and spiritual level.

All that said, it took me leaving home and going to Australia to even begin to see how differently I was raised. And ultimately, when I lived in Australia and I was on my own, working to figure out how to pay the bills, just like everyone else, I got to experience a taste of lack, scarcity, and uncertainty.

I get that it will never be the same as most of the world. I am not here to say that, at all. I know in every cell of my being, now, the immense privilege I was born into.

Ever since I started learning about entrepreneurship and having thoughts of my own business, the thing that has driven me the most is carrying on my grandparent's legacy, in multiple ways.

70 percent of people who receive an inheritance or large sums of money blow it fast. Even people who win the lottery, many of them not only blow it, but end up bankrupt. I did not and do not want to be that statistic.

When I started diving into Neuro-linguistic programming (NLP) about 15 years ago and coaching people, shifting their mindset and way of showing up in the world, I had so many of my friends tell me what an amazing manifestor I was – which was and is true. It was at that point that I decided to consciously learn what I inherently was taught my whole life.

This was before the times of the phenomenon of 'The Secret', when manifesting started to become more mainstream. I dove into every book I could find, and it has been my obsession ever since.

It has been my obsession for many reasons, but the greatest is to continue my grandparent's legacy.

I desire to grow my wealth immensely and to teach others to do the same. The reason I want to grow my wealth is because I know in every cell of my being the immense amount that we can contribute to this planet when we are financially opulent. I know the impact ONE PERSON can make when money is easily and freely flowing to you.

And that impact, that legacy, is what drives me to keep going every single day. Through all the ups and downs of life and business, I wake up every morning with the deepest desire to continue my grandparent's legacy.

All that said... even though I was living a very alternative life from my family once I moved to Australia, I still couldn't get past the way I thought I had to BE in this world.

I was constantly wanting to live up to a false ceiling of standards that were constantly changing and that I could never meet. I was wanting to make everyone in my family happy whilst living a life that most of them couldn't comprehend. I was wanting to not disappoint anyone, not share things that are meant to stay behind closed doors, whilst also trying to live into my truth.

In case you didn't' know... Being wealthy comes with a 'secret society'. Shhh... I'm gonna let you in on some of the 'secrets' in this society as we go through this book, so keep reading.

The way money and business are spoken about are very different when you have money to when you don't. And... sitting at the table with the ultra-rich brings different conversations, for sure.

THE NEW WEALTH

It's kind of an unwritten rule that what happens at those tables, stays at those tables. If the walls of country club rooms could talk... oh the stories they would tell.

It was in moving back to Denver 3.5 years ago, and a year later having my grandmother pass away, that all my work in wealth consciousness really started to land for me.

My grandmother is my biggest inspiration. She was the most amazing person in the world to me. When she passed on, my heart shattered. And also... my connection with her in some ways is stronger than ever before.

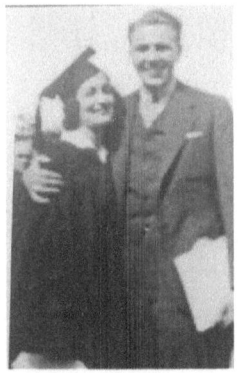

In 1938, my grandmother was one of the first 4 women to graduate from the University of Chicago with a Bachelor's Degree in Business. This is still one of the most prestigious business universities in the US to this day.

In 1968, she became the first female president of the Jewish Community Center of Chicago.

She has dedicated her life to be of service and was a revolutionary, trail-blazing woman of her time. If there was something that woman wanted, she didn't take no for an answer. Nor did my grandfather, nor does my mother, for that matter.

She and my grandfather were at multiple presidential inaugurations. I will never ever forget the way her face lit up when she would tell the story of meeting JFK at his inauguration and how he held and kissed her hand, and that she never wanted to wash her hand again.

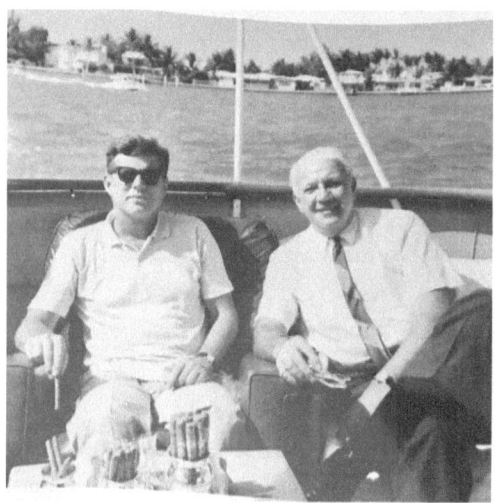

This is my grandfather on JFK's private boat when he was the President. He had invited 'Small Business' owners to meet with him and talk with him about small business in America. Small is all relative. ;-)

Eating hot dogs and smoking cigars with JFK was definitely one of the many amazing highlights of my grandfather's career and life.

I could go on and on with the inspiring stories of this amazing couple… this Empress and Emperor that have been such a massive influence in my life.

My grandfather was obviously a massive influence on my life and he died when I was 13 years young, so I have less life experience with him and also… probably because I am a woman, I have just always had such a deep admiration for my grandma.

When she passed away with almost 101 years of living in her lifetime, the world lost an amazing human. And what happened after that changed the way I knew I had to show up in this world.

For months after that, as my uncle cleared out the basement of my grandparent's home that they had lived in for 40 years, we would get picture upon picture, story upon story, articles written about my family and all of a sudden… I woke up.

There were stories I had never heard. There were stories that I lived through, but as a child, didn't realize the impact or importance and potency of.

Let me put it like this… when you grow up in an abusive home or in lack or middle class, name your situation here, that's what you know to be true.

That's why the cycle of abuse continues generationally unless a person chooses to change it. That's why poverty breeds more poverty and wealth breeds more wealth.

We are raised with certain ideas and beliefs that shape our reality and our future.

I was raised in wealth. I didn't know any different. Opulence and luxury are normal to me.

I still look at my hubby some days when my family does things or says things and say… 'Not normal, hey?'

What has been my normal with money is so different to many of you reading this book and yet as a human, I deal with the same human stuff you do. No amount of money changes that.

Whilst I have known since I left for college many years ago and got out of my super secure bubble, that my normal is not the same as others, things really landed for me in a whole new way when I started reading the stories.

The fact that I just wanted to 'fit in' and be 'normal' is one of the reasons I never shared my family stories before. I mean... the whole hero's journey... if you don't hit rock bottom, end up in 6-figure debt, etc. and climb back out... how could I be seen as successful?

I played the story in my mind, 'Keri... no one can relate to you, so why will they listen?' And then also unconsciously created a whole lot of lack and scarcity in my life in order to fit in.

I heard over and over in my mind and from people I met – 'Keri, you can't understand what it's like because you haven't experienced the hardships I have.' Which, by the way... whilst I may not have experienced extreme financial hardship, I have most certainly had my fair share of 'stuff' to deal with in my life.

Being human is being human and there is no amount of money that protects us from mental, physical and emotional abuse. But that's not what this story is about.

That said... I let these disempowering stories stop me from sharing my story with the world.

As I read the amazing stories of my family, I knew that had to end.

My grandmother would come to me over and over again and I would hear the voice in my ear... 'Kerikynns, share my story.

Kerikynns… you have created this platform… do it however you like… but share my story.'

I started to share her story but had family members not so happy about that. And so, again, it stifled my voice.

And over the past year, I have battled what it is to share this legacy. I have rumbled with wanting to honour my family and also honour myself.

So, whilst my story is different… Whilst I bring a different perspective to the world than my grandparents, the thing that still drives me every day is to continue a legacy of love and wealth and contribution.

I have realized it is my purpose on this planet to help others create and/or continue to share a legacy that is 100% purpose and soul-led and in complete alignment with you.

It was in trying to be like my family, in trying to please them and do what I THOUGHT they wanted of me, that I continually blocked myself from sharing this message with the world and doing what I know I am here to do.

And so… here we are.

The reason I am sharing my story and telling you all about where I come from is because I know what it is to live a life of opulence, this concept that many of you push away and/or don't allow yourself to receive.

I want to share this with you so that you can have a taste of it, too, and know that if it's available for me, it's available for you.

It's no surprise to me that this message comes in a time of massive change on this planet. As my grandparents were game-changers, creatives, leaders, and on the forefront of growth and change on this planet in their time, so am I.

My grandparents grew their wealth through war-times and times of depression and they constantly pulled other people up with them and asked them to play a bigger game… to look beyond their current circumstances and grow.

Today, as I sit here writing this book with people in lockdown all over the planet because of the COVID-19 virus, letting the words flow through my fingers in a time of great change on this planet… I am here to ask you to do the same.

There is a NEW WEALTH available for us right now. There is a way to show up and create your own sovereignty on this planet. This is a time of GREAT CHANGE. Many people will fall and end up in bankruptcy and economic hardship. Others will make their millions and THRIVE through this time.

My question for you is… Which one do you choose? Because creating wealth IS A CHOICE.

This book is here to help you THRIVE.

This book is a guide for you to help you make the choices and BE THE PERSON who steps into The New Wealth. Are you ready to RISE UP with me?

The time is NOW.

THE NEW WEALTH

This book, this movement, the RISE into 'The New Wealth' is for you if:

- You are wanting a new way of being in this world.
- You desire to tap into Infinite Abundance.
- You desire to live in the vibration of love.
- It's for you no matter where you are on your financial journey.
  If you are a broke spiritual healer or a multi-millionaire or anywhere in between, this will awaken you to a new level of wealth no matter where you are. I would say it would be a book to re-visit to receive the next level of activation as you strip away your next layer too.
- It's for you if you want to create a lasting legacy.
- It's for you if you are curious about 'The New Wealth' Movement.
- It's for you if you are a child/grandchild of wealth. We dive into generational wealth throughout the book.
- It's for you if you are wanting to dive deeper into multi-dimensional manifestations of wealth.
- It's for you if you are a financial advisor and want to look into the energetics of money and wealth. If you want to look at a new way of wealth that is coming our way, please turn these pages.
- It's for you if you have been through divorce and received your financial settlement but were never the one to handle the money and don't want to blow it all.
- If you have been on the awakening path and you want to drop further into your awakening… this is for you.
- This is for you if you desire to see a transference of wealth to the people vs the global elite. If you don't know what that means… read this book.
- This is for you if you are seeing the rich get richer and the poor get poorer and want to be a part of the restructuring of money to create more financial equality.

- This is for you if you want to grow your wealth. (PS- let go of any shame around being financially wealthy right now.)
- This book is for you if you are craving some 'financial security' in a time of chaos in the financial systems.
- If you want to live with Peace on Earth in your lifetime… please read this book.
- Please receive this transmission and this activation and allow yourself to be a part of this movement towards 'The New Wealth'.

This book and this movement of The New Wealth is not for you if:

- You are totally happy with where you are at in life and see all the financial systems as fair and equal.
- You live within your own sovereignty and abundance and feel totally content with life.
- You are only here to argue because you know you are right. (Step away.)
- You are totally closed minded and don't want to see any change on this planet.
- You believe the earth is flat. LOL.
- You would rather stay closed off and part of a corrupt system designed to breed fear.

Ultimately… if you are not ready to open your mind and heart to a completely new way of living on this planet, then do not read this book.

I have a grand vision for the future and many will join me in this experience of life.

If you are not willing to play a bit of make-believe with me for a bit right now… then shut this book, walk away and stay stuck in your stories of lack and limitation.

THE NEW WEALTH

But if you want to be a part of ushering in a new era of wealth and money… then turn the pages, receive this transmission, and get activated into 'The New Wealth'.

SECTION 2
THE NEW WEALTH FOUNDATIONS

In order to understand the concepts I'm going to bring to you in this book, it's important to explain a few principles to you first.

We exist in a multi-dimensional world. In this world, there is no time and space. Have you ever noticed that when you try and plan things, they don't always work according to plan?

To clarify, you set an intention to manifest something into your world and you get what you desire, but did you get there the way you thought you would? Did things come up that either created roadblocks or that created a free flow and you have no idea where the ease came from?

And why do some of those intentions become reality within minutes or days and some take years?

Have you ever noticed that sometimes a minute feels like an hour and an hour feels like a minute?

That's because there is no time and space. Nothing is linear. It is what we make it.

When you start to look at yourself as a multi-dimensional being, you open yourself up to freedom. A freedom that exists for all of us when we choose to tap into it.

THE NEW WEALTH

In this quantum reality, there are multiple versions of the same timeline happening at the same time.

Consider it this way…

Maybe you are out with friends or family and have a great night. You get home and start talking about the amazingness of your time together and your stories don't quite match up. It doesn't't even make sense, because you were both in that same place together but remember different experiences, and wonder how you missed what they are saying happened. You may even disagree with what you both saw, both of you totally knowing and convinced that what you saw is the REAL thing that happened.

Check out something called the Mandela Effect. It's when people experience a certainty that something happened in history, but it didn't happen that way.

Is it your memory that creates this? Maybe it's that you were in different parallel realities and both are true. What is true?

Maybe you get the concept of different dimensions, maybe you don't. However, in order to open to achieving The New Wealth, you get to believe they exist. In my experience, I would encourage you to trust the existence of alternative dimensions.

Also, for the sake of this book and to understand being a multi-dimensional being, know that we have multiple bodies. We have an emotional, energetic, a spiritual, a physical, a mental body and an astral body.

When you want to become a sovereign being and the master of your destiny, you will have the ability to create instant manifestation. It's crucial to know about and have a relationship with each of your bodies and nurture them all. We will talk more about this later.

Humanity as a whole has been living in a three-dimensional (3D) reality. In this reality, we have human bodies. We are in physical form. In purely 3D reality, it is a linear time frame. You believe that things go from one point to the next.

In this 3D reality, things are black and white. Both space and time exist in a linear time frame. Point A to point B with limited understanding of creation, which is the mystery.

We live in very masculine energy full of lack, fear, limitations, and control. We live in the very limited 1% of existence in this current 3D reality.

When we move to the 5D, we find the 99%, which points to creation and a solution beyond the 3D.

In the 5D reality, we live in expansion. Time and space don't exist so instant manifestation is 100% possible.

The energy is love, joy, bliss, abundance, and peace.

Everyone is acknowledged for their gifts and everyone gets to feel fulfilled as they live their purpose on the planet.

Peace prevails.

It truly is the land of Freedom through Unity.

I know many of you are probably thinking this is BS and saying that I am full of shit and living in some fairytale land of make-believe. Well, maybe that's true. And if it is, I ask that you challenge yourself and come and join me in the land of the 'crazy' and enjoy this paradise with us.

It really is as simple as this... *What you look for, you will receive.*

And you know how powerful your mind is, right? *What you think about, you get.*

So, if you live in a world where you are trained to think about debt, fear, retaliation, eye for an eye, I'm better than you, a totally segregated world of power, control, greed and manipulation, then guess what you will get? More and more of that! A vicious loop in consciousness.

Consciousness, as I speak of it here, is Awareness.

Collective Consciousness is the Awareness of the Greater Whole.

So whilst there are a select few of us on the planet already awakening to this other dimension, this other way of BEing on the planet, there are billions more who are not. And so the collective consciousness is currently living in the 3D reality because that is what we have been programmed to believe is the only reality for thousands of years.

Know the lights are getting turned on and we are being guided to know there is another way. There is another way.

Perhaps, for many of you reading this, it may be hard to wrap your head around. However, the faster you do, the faster you will find yourself living in a different reality, in The New Wealth.

Keri Norley

This energetic change is coming. So, please sit yourself down, turn these pages and dive into this Awakening.

Hang with me until the end. I'm going to show you the way.

If you're feeling tingling and anticipatory and even electric, or maybe you are peaceful and calm, or maybe you don't feel anything at all... either way, you are in the right place to take your life to another dimension.

It's an honour to guide you there.

CELEBRATE THE TRIGGERS

I'm guessing if you're reading this book and hang with me long enough, at some point I will trigger you. And if it's not me, it will be someone.

I want to bring this to the conversation right up front, because if you don't really get what's happening at that point in which you get triggered, you may want to run from this concept of 'The New Wealth, from this message, and it's too important for you to hear and embody for me to not speak to this right away.

Even if you think you know what I am talking about when it comes to triggers, please read on.

This is important.

On this path, you will meet resistance as you move forward. This resistance looks like triggers. Emotions such as feeling angry, frustrated, frozen, and/or a mess may come up for you. These emotions and triggers can make you feel like you will want to stop you dead in your tracks. It can pull you off the path of abundance and wealth.

The inclination for many people is to blame the messenger that triggered you and/or give up. You may want to give up on your soul's purpose and sometimes even life itself.

That's the time you get to dig deeper and look at what is triggering you.

A trigger is something you will want to conceal. It's like a little hidden mystery that doesn't't want to be seen because it hurts. You will feel vulnerable to look at that place inside of you, so you will create that trigger to keep you from diving deeper because that feels safer for your ego.

The thing is, it's the truth behind that trigger that is your conduit to shifting your energy and moving out of fear and into love. It is a gateway.

Looking at what is actually creating the emotional trigger in you, whatever that is, and making peace with it, loving that part of yourself, is a crucial piece of transformation and your ascension and embodiment of your dreams.

A trigger is a gift.

When you get triggered, celebrate.

And before you go and throw your blaming, finger-pointing, hurtful words back at the person who is triggering you, look at yourself.

Look at WHY that brings up the emotions that it does and then look under that. What little treasure is sitting there for you to love?

Imagine it like this...

Your little prince/princess does or witnesses something uncomfortable that creates an emotional reaction. You store that reaction away in a little internal jail cell at the bottom of the dungeon because it's just too hard to deal with. It's likely that little part of you has been locked away for a very long time.

So when you get triggered, take a moment to go and look at that jail cell, talk to your little inner prince/princess. How, or in what situation, did that trigger get planted there? Why? And then ask yourself, 'What can you do to simply let that prisoner out of the cell?'

Then, take a moment to forgive yourself and the others involved for putting yourself into that jail cell.

Now that the jail cell is empty and that part of you is free, consider what you will put into that empty space. When there is an empty space it will be filled, so choose wisely. I suggest that you fill it with love.

The more pockets of love that you plant within yourself, the higher vibrational you become.

Be kind to yourself through this process. Please keep coming back to this and reminding yourself how to truly take full responsibility for your own reactions.

Whether it be in this book that I say something that triggers you or it's in your day-to-day life, every trigger is an opportunity to love yourself more. It's an opportunity to step into unity with yourself and create your own Sovereignty.

I want to give you a tool to help you move through triggers. Knowing that our triggers are stored in our body, a really great way to move through them is to move your body.

One of my favourite and most impactful tools to move energy is Quantum Flow.

I have my first gift for you… It's a video that you can engage with and DO some Quantum Flow to help you quickly shift your energy and remove that stuck energy/emotion in your body. Please go check out this beautiful gift and use it. Use it often. Get involved in the amazing Quantum Flow familia. It has the power to change your life.

https://kerinorley.com/resources

Speaking of triggers… In this book, I am an American/Aussie author. Some of my words are American, some are Australian. Neither are right or wrong. Honestly, I cannot remember which is for which country so I just write and assume that if there is a 'u' put into colour but I use an American spelling of something else, it just is and it is ok.

Think of it as one of my funny quirks. You will hear it in my accent and you can see it in my writing.

I know some of you out there are grammatical fanatics. It's all good. I'm a smart woman who knows what I am talking about, don't let mix-matched languages mean anything other than that.

Awesome! So now that we have gotten some important principles opened up for thought here, we can move on to the deep dive exploration of 'The New Wealth'.

SECTION 3
AN OVERVIEW OF OUR CURRENT FINANCIAL SYSTEM

We are in one of the most unprecedented times in history. As I write this, we are finally starting to see things open up after 2.5 months of being stuck in our homes in lockdown because of the Coronavirus.

- People who have thrown their energy and savings into businesses are struggling to make it through.
- Businesses that have taken years to build are closing down.
- People are losing jobs.
- The governments are printing trillions of dollars to bail out people.
- People are living in fear that is being spread like wildfire by the media and government.
- People are being isolated and told to cover their faces, cover their identity and wear masks.
- The media is being censored more than ever before.
- Our 'health care' (or as I like to say… our 'sick care') system is being questioned.
- People are starting to see the financial industry for what it is.
- Marriages will have gotten stronger or broken down in this time.
- Family values are being questioned.
- Suicide rate is up.

THE NEW WEALTH

We are at war. This is a different kind of war than the ones of guns and violence, although that is here now too, with the riots taking over cities all over America.

We are at war with the powers that be.

We are waking up and seeing the systems collapsing.

The 'health care' system, the financial systems and the school systems are all falling down around us.

We are having our rights taken from us. The right to freedom of speech is definitely not there, as people who are bringing truths that the powers that be don't want you to see are getting accounts completely shut down.

The thought of mandatory vaccination has people who even traditionally believe in vaccinations up in arms. It's opening an entirely new conversation about the safety of vaccines in a world that has been so divided in the past.

And as I sit here writing this book, riots are breaking out all around the US in the rally for #BlackLivesMatter to bring equality to black lives.

The way we have lived life until now is crumbling around us, and whilst it's a challenging time for all of us, it is a beautiful sight to behold.

The truths are being revealed.

People and institutions that many of us have put blind faith into are starting to wake up to the corruptness of the leaders of this current world. We can't turn a blind eye to the money-hungry corporations taking advantage of the people they are meant to be serving.

It's time to wake up and see what has been under your nose for decades. It's time to take ownership of your life and stop giving your power away.

It's time to change the power on this planet.

It's time to bring it home to the people.

It's time to rise above the chaos and anarchy and supremacy that has kept the super-elite making more and more money and taking it from you, the ones who are working so diligently to make ends meet, to save your money, to grow your wealth.

It's time to become a part of the change that you wish to see in this world.

It's time for The New Wealth.

Right now, in this massive time of change, we are moving into a new consciousness on this planet. We are completely leaping timelines, we are in different dimensions and we are raising the vibrations of the planet.

In order for me to help you shift into The New Wealth paradigm, I must start with explaining our current financial system to you, because when you see this, I'm guessing you will begin to see how manipulated and controlled we have been and how the financial system isn't here to support us. It is here to support the global financial elite.

And when you deeply get this, I'm guessing, like me, you will want to be a part of the change. You will realize how important this time in the world is to completely rise above this way of BEing on the planet.

THE NEW WEALTH

It is our time. Together, we will rise.

Truthfully, this topic is so big and deep and full of corruption that I don't even know where to begin. Also, please know I am NOT a financial advisor and this is not financial 'advice'. My expertise is not in economics and the ins and outs of the financial industry.

My brilliance is in energetic and emotional clearing, reading the energy of everything, playing in the quantum realms and understanding the human psyche, but in order for this to make the greatest impact for you, it's critical to share this information.

In this section, it is my hope to bring you enough information to have you want to go look for more, for you to do your own research. It is my intention to peel back the curtains enough to have you look deeper and make informed choices about your own financial destiny.

NOTHING in this book is giving you advice on what to do with your money. Speak to a financial advisor for that. Everything in this book is to open you up to a new reality that we all have the ability to choose.

It's easier to accept where we are heading when you get why where we are isn't working.

Please know that whatever I share, there is more to the story. If this awakens you and angers you, then congrats. Feel free to go and take the time to do your own research. It's all right there for you to read about or listen to.

Speaking of listening to more and educating yourself more... I have interviewed a legend in this space of finance in The New Wealth to bring you some more critical information around the reality of our current financial system.

Please take the time to listen to the brilliance of Rossco Paddison as he distills this down for you in a way that will blow your mind.

There is also another video that is by Christof Melchizedek that will open your mind to a whole new way of looking at the current reality of the world. I get fired up every time I hear it or him speak.

Please take the time to listen to BOTH of these amazing men and allow yourself to expand beyond where you are currently thinking.

https://kerinorley.com/resources

As you read this, as you listen to the interviews included in this book, as you do the activations, please tell others. Help spread the message around a new way of doing wealth and money in the world.

Share this book with others.

Have book clubs about it.

Do whatever it takes to awaken humanity to the control and manipulation we have been under and together we can rise above this all and create 'The New Wealth'.

Ok. Let's get into it.

OUR CURRENT REALITY

Let's start with what we, as a collective consciousness, currently believe in, stand for and value in this 3D reality: (This is under the premise of the current perception of reality in June, 2020.)

- A corrupt government filled with people who are there for their own personal interests.
- A financial system that has set us up to be in debt forever and is making money off of you every single day.
- A health care system that keeps people sick and is financially winning. The more sick people get, and the 'needier' of pharmaceuticals humanity becomes, the more we create a humanity that is addicted to medications and trapped in cycles of bad health. Consequently, the pharmaceutical companies get richer and richer.
- Racism, prejudice, and discrimination due to sex, religion and skin colour.
- Fear.
- Lack and scarcity.
- Child and sex trafficking.
- Domestic violence.
- Destroying the earth with non-renewable resources.
- Collusion. Money buying power.
- Police brutality.
- Over-crowded prisons.
- Hate.
- Persecution.
- Gun violence.
- Anti-Semitism
- Terrible education systems that teach kids to be robots in order to get a job but not think for themselves or be equipped to actually handle life.
- And so much more.

As a collective, this is the energy and consciousness of the majority of the planet. This is what we have created for ourselves.

Throughout this whole book, please remember everything is a mirror of yourself. What we see in our external reality is a direct mirror of our internal consciousness.

If you were to really take ownership of what that means, you would hear me say that **we imagined this reality**, at some level. We created this. And when we look at it that way, it's so empowering because if we created this, we can create something else. And at this moment in time, that is what is happening.

We are in the midst of a mass Awakening. Congratulations for being here at this time on the planet. It's an amazing and historical moment to be alive and to live through.

We have a choice right now. We can continue to buy into these conditions that no one actually wants to be a part of, OR we can choose The New Earth and The New Wealth and re-create our lives on planet Earth.

THE NEW WEALTH

THE CURRENT FINANCIAL SYSTEM

Let's dive deeper into the Current Financial System.

We are going to go really 'big picture' thinking here so take a walk with me.

I want to start with talking about the US Central Banking System, The Federal Reserve System.

The Federal Reserve Banking System is the Central Bank of the United States. It was created in 1913 by Congress to provide the nation with a more flexible, safer and more stable financial and monetary system.

Ultimately, The Federal Reserve System is not private, and until this year has not been regulated by the government. It is independent of everything, which gives the bank its own power.

It is responsible for conducting the nation's monetary policies, supervising and regulating banks and other financial institutions, maintaining the stability of the financial system and providing financial services to the US government and US financial institutions, as well as playing a major role in operating the nation's payment systems.

OK. What the heck does all that mean?

This is a banking system that is not part of the government but not privately owned either, so is held accountable to no one and has control of the flow of money.

They can print more, or hold back, or move the interest rates up until they hit the debt ceiling that has been set by Congress, who can move the ceiling up at any time they need more money. As long as it is under the debt ceiling, The Fed makes these choices and are held accountable to no one.

Let that sink in.

The Fed Chair is required to report to Congress, but it is said in the quote right below that the Federal Reserve Board does not require approval from anyone else...

'In addition, though the Congress sets the goals for monetary policy, decisions of the Board—and the Fed's monetary policy-setting body, the Federal Open Market Committee—about how to reach those goals do not require approval by the President or anyone else in the executive or legislative branches of government.' https://www.federalreserve.gov/faqs/about_14986.htm

Not only that, the President appoints the Federal Reserve Chair. Let that sink in.

So the leader of the Western world now has the power to appoint the person who is going to make all the financial decisions that do not require approval from anyone else.

Phhhwaaaoh… whhhhoooaa. Right?

At this point, I ask you to question that if this is the truth, which it is, how do you feel about our financial system being regulated by a select few people who actually do not have to 'report' to anyone about their actions?

Money keeps getting printed, interest rates are controlled, our livelihood can go up and down at the decision of a select few – who, by the way – are being led by corruption.

THE NEW WEALTH

Something that leaders and Presidents of the past have tried to do is to change this structure and have the Fed be part of the government. It's not been allowed because the people didn't want the Fed to be making choices because their 'boss', the President, wanted it to be done.

JFK tried to merge the Fed and The Treasury and was shot 6 months later. Maybe that is just a coincidence?

It has never happened until recently, during the Coronavirus lockdown, President Trump passed a law that the Fed is now run by The Treasury, which is run by the President.

So now, officially, the president controls the Central Bank. Which leads us to the concept of Trump nationalizing the Federal Reserve.

Over the years, there has been collusion and corruption between the central banks of other countries to come together to control the financial system of the world. Global financial markets have been dependent on these Central Banks and are in debt to them. Effectively, in debt to the Global Financial Elite.

We have been in a 'globalized economy', which describes an interdependence of nations around the globe fostered through free trade. This is great for the sharing of ideas and trades between countries and more. It also can be problematic in times of a downturn in any country's economy because of the domino effect it has globally.

And another big problem with globalization is that our local businesses and people can be affected by sending the work to other countries that can do it cheaper. The other side of this being that developing countries are having more industry and work brought to their country.

It also supports the corporate elite to buy out competitors around the world and gain more power and wealth.

So Trump taking the Fed into the Treasury is taking it away from the corrupt global financial elite and bringing it into US control. I'm not here to pick sides on which is best for us. I'm just here to give you a big picture idea.

Again, we are in unprecedented times with economies shifting. Time will tell what happens.

There's an interesting video that will give you a bit more to think about in relationship to this massive shift in power on the resources page I have created for you. Check it out here: http://www.kerinorley.com/resources

So, what does that all mean to you?

There is a lot at play when it comes to our creation and distribution of money that maybe you didn't know. Maybe this is an eye-opening moment when you begin to realize that we are living in a corrupt system rigged for the global elite, or maybe you were already open to this information.

Either way is perfect.

Remember, the intention for this section of the book is simply to bring awareness to a banking system that really isn't designed for the people at all.

Remember to go and check out the videos with Rossco Paddison and Christof Melchidezek who dives deeper into this system.

www.kerinorley.com/resources

And then continue to do your own research.

TRUMP AND SHADOW

Before we go on to our DEBT-BASED financial system… I want to make a little side note since we are talking about Trump.

Let me start this by reminding you of one of the foundations of The New Wealth that I spoke about in the last chapter, 'Celebrate Your Triggers'. If you are triggered by even having Trump's name mentioned in this book, please, allow yourself to keep reading.

Truthfully, I have debated putting this piece into the book, because I don't want you to stop reading here at the mention of his name. This book and message are too important for that. As I said in the last chapter, we get to celebrate our triggers, so with that said, please read on with an open mind.

I've been having some big conversations lately about the role President Trump is playing in the world right now that I feel is quite relevant to share with you here.

Before I even begin to share these thoughts, please know this is NOT a political debate. I am not picking sides on this. I'm just going to ask you to expand your field about the role this man is playing in our world right now.

I'm not going to be the person to use bad words or energy towards our president, and please know that I see everything you see.

And it's because of all the 'flaws' that piss everyone off about the man, that he is creating such a very strong reflection for everyone on this planet to look within themselves and heal that part of themselves that has been hurt by this behavior in the past.

President Trump is showing us all the shadowy parts of ourselves and also all the shadowy parts of the structures we have in place around the world, as well as the consciousness of this planet that is archaic and no longer serves us.

Humanity is waking up and seeing how much we dislike the 3D template of struggle that we live in. We are waking up to see the racism, womanizing, abuse, lack, control, manipulation, anti-semitism, etc... He makes it so in our faces that we finally get to come together as humanity and be angry enough to want to make a change.

This is SHADOW WORK. President Trump is doing one heck of a job being a reflection for us to see all the places that trigger us and get us moving, so that we can choose to break down this consciousness, take a stand for something better, and ultimately raise the consciousness of the planet.

This is the work for ALL of us, personally and globally, to be looking within and seeing the places we don't want to see, and loving all of ourselves so that we can choose differently.

So, whether any one of us likes that man or not, and we all have many reasons to not like him. He has also done things that have been good for us, passed some amazing policies and somehow the economy is stronger than it's been in years. No matter the politics of this or our feelings about him, he is an important leader of our time.

In the history books, this will be looked upon as an amazing time of transformation on this planet and structures crumbling, and Donald Trump is a critical piece to the inevitable unraveling that is currently happening right now.

Trump is very good at using chaos to create new policies and move them through quickly, as we saw with the Fed and others.

I see some of the policies he is bringing into place right now and celebrate him, and some make me want to storm the white house myself, I see his behavior and want to look the other way (like you, I'm sure).

That said… I don't envy any of the global leaders right now, especially Trump. We are in unprecedented times and there is no rulebook with what to do.

I get the energy it takes to hold the mirror for the shadow, because that is what I do for my clients. It takes strength and conviction in who you are to be able to hold the mirror for people to see the shadow because it requires that you don't fall into it with them, so that they (or we) can see it for themselves and transmute it into love.

So for Trump to be a global anchor for this, takes quite a thick skin, of which he has. And we can all throw daggers his way or we can realize he's representing a system that most of us in humanity want to move away from, that has been this way for thousands of years, and that by seeing it in him, we get to heal it within ourselves and across the planet so that we can rise above it.

I want to share this here because it helps to see this whole corrupt system for what it is… And these systems that we buy into fall into the shadows, filled with murky, controlling, manipulative ways.

Ok, so now that you get the shadowy aspects of everything going on here, keep coming along with me…

WE HAVE A FINANCIAL SYSTEM BASED ON DEBT

If you want someone to do something, the best way to teach it is through your own actions. As the saying goes… actions speak louder than words.

So let's look at our economy and debt from the top. When the US government needs money, they look to the Federal Reserve and ask for money.

From 2007 to 2017 the US debt rose from around $9 trillion to $20 trillion dollars. The US Treasury borrowed money from the Fed and the Fed 'printed' it. Meaning, they gave access to a bunch of numbers in a computer for the Treasury to do what they will.

The US ends up in more debt.

Please take a moment to consider the rescue money that has been given away to the people of America for COVID relief. The US government has given relief to families and businesses because of the lack of ability to work. Trillions of dollars has been created out of thin air already, within weeks. This massive relief funding has happened in countries around the world.

From a modeling perspective for all of humanity…. We are in a DEBT CONSCIOUSNESS.

From the top down, money is being borrowed, always living in debt. Trillions of dollars of debt which, as of 2019, equates to $161,022 worth of debt per US taxpayer, according to Forbes. Some of this debt is borrowed from Social Security, so the government is borrowing against your pension.

Really… how are trillions of dollars going to get paid off? And what does that even mean? This is a currency that has nothing

THE NEW WEALTH

backing it, and within a made-up system. The banks sit with all our money within their control and get to make compounding interest off of that every day.

The compounding interest that is available for the banks is off of our 'hard-earned dollar'.

Compounding interest can be thought of as "interest on interest." So it compounds when you put your initial amount of money into the bank and then make interest on it and then you make interest on the initial sum of money plus the interest earned.

When you have interest compounding daily, you can make a lot more than if you have simple interest calculated quarterly or yearly. The banks make money by holding our money and making interest on it. Then they also turn around and charge us banking fees.

> SIDE NOTE: Hint hint... you may want to look for opportunities that can get YOU compounding interest and not give that opportunity away to the banks. And yes, there are some opportunities for you to check out that will give YOU compounding interest at the back of the book, so please make sure to take a look.

Now, maybe you can see that money and wealth is rigged for governments and for the big banks.

Have you ever looked around to notice it?

Have you ever noticed that we 100% live in a debt consciousness?

People wonder why they have so many problems with debt. We are trained to be in debt and then shamed for doing what we were taught in actions.

And yet, this is our current reality. This is the banking system that we are so afraid will collapse and are so trusting towards.

Keri Norley

PAPER DOLLAR, DOLLAR BILLS Y'ALL. IS IT OF ANY VALUE?

Now, let's talk about our current currency no longer backed by gold, or anything, for that matter. There are some people out there that don't realize this.

Our currency, the money we spend every day is not backed by anything. It's about as useful as handing over a piece of paper and saying, 'I'll give you this $1 and you'll believe it's worth something.'

And yet, we still give it power. We still trust that it is of value and means something.

It has power because that is what we currently have as a measure of 'value' or currency. And, as shown over the years, that value could be measured in gold, in cacao beans, in barter and trade, etc. There have been so many forms of currency over the existence of this planet and they only work because we put our trust into the system and use that value of exchange.

THE NEW WEALTH

As people have reviewed this before going to print there was a question that has come up that I will answer.

> *** Keri, if your family created success in this banking system and you are a product of 'financial elite', how can you be saying this?
>
> A few reasons…
>
> 1. There is 'financial elite' and 'Financial Elite'. Within the 1% there is a wide range of wealth.
>
>   There is a 'ranking' of wealth. Really, it's based on the opulence of millions of dollars that a person is 'worth'.
>
>   It's important to realize that just because a person has millions of dollars that does not mean that they are out of this system that is still globally corrupt by the financial elite.
>
>   The global financial elite are the ones that have accumulated wealth beyond the billionaires, like the Richard Bransons and Warren Buffets of the world. Their wealth is too beyond measure to be calculated for the public.
>
>   And so yes… whilst I was raised in a family that has amassed wealth in this economy and banking system, they are not the ones controlling and manipulating the system. We are just as in it as you.
>
> 2. Yes, my family amassed massive wealth in this banking system. It has been 'good' for us. There is no doubt about it. And I'm grateful for that every day.

And now, we can create a different reality. It doesn't mean that what we have had as a banking system didn't work for the time we have had it. We are always doing the best we can with the tools that we have available.

For example: When we had a horse and buggy, we were grateful for wheels to transport us. Eventually we evolved into having cars. The cars are amazing and who would want to go back to horse and carriage, right? But does that negate that in the era of horse and carriage, that wasn't amazing for them?

No! It was amazing for the time.

In the same way that the banking system that we have has supported us and helped some of us grow wealth and some of us take on debt. It has been perfect for our time, just like the horse and carriage was perfect for its time.

And now… we get to do it another way.

3. Just because it works for one person doesn't mean it will work for another.

   One of the hardest things I have had to untangle in shifting my relationship with money and wealth is not doing the same thing as my family and feeling the pressure of that.

   There are certain expectations to live up to when you are raised in wealth and I have been questioned… would your grandfather want you to do that? Would your grandfather do it that way? And I have asked myself those questions thousands of times.

THE NEW WEALTH

> And then I have struggled to do my work in the world with the pressure of doing it like him, be like him, making decisions like him, when he was born in 1907.
>
> The times were so different when he grew his business and we have all evolved. The human species has evolved, technology has evolved. So much has changed over the years that it's not even a direct comparison and so I have had to learn that I get to do it my way.
>
> I get to leave my legacy the way I choose and each step still honour and love my grandparents for the opportunities that they have created for me by being born into this family.
>
> So yes, it worked for them and in some ways still works for me. That doesn't mean that I don't see a new way forward.

Right now, we are currently bridging two realities, and so for the time being the banking system is in place and we can use it for what it is, and begin to look for alternative ways to hold our wealth.

Like I said when I started this section… this is only a taste of what is happening on a global level in our financial system. What have you taken away from this so far?

Does it get you fired up realizing that the financial system is designed to keep us in debt and to live in fear and to constantly be giving our money to the global Financial Elite?

Do yourself a favour and go and do some research around the global financial elite and who is in bed running the banks and how much power they have. It will open your eyes to a whole new world.

I bring this basic overview to the table here and now because we have all been asking for a change in the financial system. Over the years, as the rich get richer and the poor get poorer and that gap gets bigger, it is in my heart that we are able to change that and create a system that brings power to the people and more financial equality to the world.

What would happen if we had a unified currency that knew no borders and did not discriminate by race, religion, or where you are born?

What would happen if there was a way to bring people our own financial sovereignty?

What would it be like for the PEOPLE of the world to get to have the privilege of compounding interests working FOR US instead of the banks getting the compounding interest on our 'hard-earned money'?

This is where The New Wealth is taking us.

To a new form of currency, to a new era FOR the people.

Imagine a world where our currency is equal, and we have equal opportunity.

Imagine a world where our money is always working for us.

Imagine how different your life would be now if you had money that was always working for you.

And if we weren't fighting over money and power, we could have a consciousness of love and peace.

This is the world I want to live in.

THE NEW WEALTH

This is the new reality coming for us.

We get to CHOOSE this.

I invite you to take a moment now to close your eyes, take a few deep breaths in and see yourself in a world of Infinite Abundance. I know your mental mind might be struggling to believe you right now, but just pretend that Infinite Abundance, Love, Peace and Vitality on Earth is all possible and then:

- Feel how good it feels to live in this abundance;
- Take a look around you and see what you see;
- Have a listen and what do you hear?
- Can you smell anything?
- Taste anything?

Use all of your senses right now to experience yourself in this reality of 'The New Wealth'.

Now… really do it. Close your eyes and do the thing.

Ok… did you do it? Yes?

Awesome.

So if you can do this… if you can imagine 'The New Wealth', then it's possible.

Everything you create in your life first starts with the thought that it's possible.

If you can imagine it, it is 100% possible, so now keep reading along as we walk through stepping into 'The New Wealth'.

REVIEW

- We live in a corrupt financial system that is ruled by the Global Financial Elite.

- We live in debt and slavery consciousness and it is disempowering to the people of the world.

- We are already living in a digital currency system in that there are not as many bills/coins produced in the world as there is money in our bank accounts.

- We get to look at our own shadows, fears, lack and scarcity so that we can create a change that is going to bring us to Abundance, Joy, Love, Bliss and Peace.

- Please go out and do your own research in this space. Open your mind to what is going on and be willing to take a stand for creating financial Sovereignty in The New Wealth.

ACTIVATION QUESTIONS:

1. Where are you intrigued to dive into further after reading and listening to this section?

   Please remember to listen to Rossco and Christof's videos too. They are so enlightening. We talk about so much more than I can get to here. They are both very different and I highly recommend you take the time to watch them both. Find them both here at www.kerinorley.com/resources.

2. How do you feel about our financial system after reading that? Check in with yourself and really listen. How do you feel?

3. What got triggered in you as you read this?

4. What is the consciousness of our current reality? What is the consciousness of the reality we are moving towards?

   Please, discuss this with friends. What would happen if you opened yourself even more fully to this conversation of where we can collectively call in 'The New Wealth'?

   And what would happen if you just began to live this reality and you all held each other accountable to this abundance that is here for you?

5. Ask yourself, 'What is the next aligned action to take?', and write that here and then DO IT.

   Don't be that person that reads this book, answers the questions and then doesn't do the action. #dothething

6. Please remember to do the visualisation of yourself in 'The New Wealth'. Keep experiencing yourself there, as often as you can.

   One day… you will wake up pinching yourself that you are there.

SECTION 4
WHAT DOES IT MEAN TO MAGNETIZE ABUNDANCE?

At the truest form of this… To magnetize true abundance through LOVE on demand is to live an orgasmic life. Yup… leave it to me to go right there. There is no dancing around this. It is what it is.

I'm for real. And if talking about orgasms in a book about wealth triggers you, I invite you to look into this trigger and why you have stuff around that.

Whether you are triggered or not, keep reading. We are getting juicy. ;-)

For a long time, I have not spoken about pleasure publicly. Until sitting here writing this, I never really thought about why.

But it would have been the fear of being scorned publicly for talking about money and orgasm in the same breath. That's certainly not PROPER according to the 'Miss Manners' way that I was raised.

But I can't let what others think about me hold me back from sharing absolute magic and the most wonderful way of living. That would be terrible for all of you that will read this book and change your life.

THE NEW WEALTH

> Side note: If you want to magnetize your paying tribe to you, you are going to have to be ok with pissing people off and not being for everyone so that you can cut through the noise and allow your tribe to find you and have them love you.

It's your job to walk this path of ascension and show others the way. We are in this together. Those who do not rise up will be left behind.

You must learn to vibrate at this new level of LOVE and PEACE and ABUNDANCE as we land The New Wealth.

Isn't that horrible? (Do you hear my sarcasm? ;-))

Do you realize that in order to be the most magnetic version of yourself, you get to be the most aligned, loving, beautiful, sexy, abundant, rich AF, orgasmic, blissful version of yourself?

Everything you do gets to feel good.

And that is the ultimate secret to Instant Manifestation.

So what does orgasm have to do with being magnetic?

Orgasm is the ultimate pleasure and unlocking yourself through orgasm aligns your energetic current.

Plus, when you orgasm, you are at the point of creation. So you can call in your dreams at the point of creation.

BTW- orgasm with a partner or self-pleasure. Either way allows you to run that magnetic current within your field.

And if you have no idea what I am talking about and want to dive into more of this concept start looking into it. I know this can be a touchy subject and this book is not the space to dive deep into this, but really what I want to invite you into is the thought that your life gets to be FULL OF PLEASURE.

It gets to be orgasmic. Orgasmic being that current that runs through you, which you can experience with or without penetration.

This is why sitting and praying whilst looping in the same old patterns over and over again for years and hoping a bag of money will fall on your head isn't really working for you in your 3D world of limitations.

I am here to help you move beyond those limitations and see how to magnetize abundance.

To magnetize abundance is to live a life of true pleasure and do what you are meant to do on this planet.

You are here for a purpose. A purpose that only you can fulfill in this thread of life. And it's in answering every single call of your soul that you are being Divinely led and co-creating with the greater consciousness, and so unquestionably magnetizing everything you desire into your life.

Now, you have a choice…

You can remain in the third dimension (3D) disconnected from your higher self and bang your head against a wall trying to move ahead in a system that is crumbling, or you can choose your own Divinity.

Your own self-sovereignty. Your own Self-Mastery.

And when you truly look at yourself and into all of your shadowy places, always holding a mirror up to yourself and always going within whilst simultaneously choosing the light, choosing abundance, choosing bliss, choosing love... that is when you can begin to be your own sovereign being.

That is when you begin to become truly magnetic.

So, Why Aren't You Here Yet?

You force it. You brutalize it. You beat it. You push it. You try and control it whilst simultaneously fearing the exact thing that you desire.

Your beliefs and your energy will continue to push it away 'cause you have not actually done the inner work to see the dis-empowering beliefs.

You believe that inherently you are not good enough or knowledgeable enough or smart enough or strong enough, etc., to stand in your dreams. At some level you believe that someone is one day going to appoint you King or Queen of your dreams.

Why aren't you magnetizing that which you desire?

Because you don't let yourself.

Because you continue looping in your patterns and no matter what you do, you keep banging your head against the same damn wall. You may even have an amazingly abundant and wonderful life and can still be playing the same frustrating stories out, just with a new situation and a more easeful, abundant way of life.

By the way, looping, self-sabotaging behaviors don't discriminate by money. Multi-millionaires loop and get in their own way too.

So today, make the choice to ascend beyond your current reality. Everything I am about to share with you starts with a decision.

HOW TO MAGNETIZE ABUNDANCE

Step One: DECIDE

A DECISION IS TO CUT OFF FROM ALL OTHER POSSIBILITY.

- Decide that you are no longer willing to play the un-joyful, empty way of life. - Decide that you are not going to let fear stop you from anything. - Decide that you are going to go all in on following your soul and your life will change.

New things will show up in your field to show you that you are on the right path. You will begin to feel more joy and bliss and love and abundance, and the world will keep reflecting it back, and then it only gets better and better and better, every day of your life.

Step Two: BECOME SOVEREIGN

WHAT DOES BEING YOUR OWN SOVEREIGN BEING ACTUALLY MEAN? AND WHY IS IT IMPORTANT?

As we move into The New Wealth, the power will come back from those that are currently in power, and manipulating and controlling the population, to the individual.

We are seeing so much of this as we go through this Coronavirus experience. For example, Bill Gates and Fauci pushing choices onto the people that mean that they get financial gain.

Umm… really? You get a choice!

We the people get to choose what we put into our bodies. Period.

THE NEW WEALTH

It's so important that we, as individuals, see through this control and manipulation through those in power and the media. The more of us that wake up and stand together against the abuse of our human rights, the greater the shift in consciousness of the collective and the greater impact we make.

It's great to witness that more and more people are waking up to the fact that the ones we thought had our best interest at heart were truly using their influence for their own personal agenda all along. Be it monetary gains, influence gains, power gains, sexual exploitation… you name it, most of the people who are creating the rules we have been living by are living in their ego and their limited 3D mind, and totally in it for their own personal gains.

It sucks. We are being controlled and manipulated by people who are living in a trance state in a limited mind.

Billions of people, maybe you up until now, are blindly following these lies and remaining stuck in the fear that is spreading like wildfire through the media.

Everything we are told is really a lie. We are controlled and manipulated so that those on the top can remain in power and we are drip-fed the info that the powers that be want us to hear so that we stay in a trance of disempowerment and they can control us.

As you take the journey through this book, I invite you to expand yourself beyond what you know to be true and just remain open-minded.

As we ascend into The New Wealth, into a paradigm that is the vibration of Love and Joy and Bliss and Abundance, the people whose vibrations cannot rise up, or they will explode, are leaving Earth right now.

We are having a wave of mass destruction because Mother Gaia is self-correcting for this move into the 5D.

This is not to say that I don't feel for the humanness of this and the great loss going on right now, in all the ways. I do.

I just get that this is far bigger than a virus and whatever else comes our way in these next couple years as the systems collapse.

I get that this is an energetic correction. Those that cannot energetically cross this bridge are going to leave the planet over these next few years.

There is nothing we can do to stop this. It is what must happen, with all the love in the world.

I say that knowing that it means that I may lose people in my life, too, and either way… whatever happens, it is our destiny. It is what we chose when we made an agreement to descend down to this Earthly plane at this time.

Some of us will leave now to go and help from the astral planes to energetically bring in this new vibration. That is their destiny.

Right now, it's your job to focus on raising your vibration to allow yourself into the 5D and living here more and more and more.

We are bridging the worlds right now.

It's why some days you can feel absolutely in flow, on fire, unstoppable (5D reality). Then the next day you are feeling like

THE NEW WEALTH

you fell under a bag of bricks and you are trying to run through mud and getting all sludgy and stuck, and can't move with ease and everything feels hard and frustrating.

We haven't fully bridged into the new earth yet. And so we are currently in each reality simultaneously.

Really… it's a mindfuck. I know. It's not easy to get your head around this.

And it's because of this energetic shift that is happening on this planet that it's absolutely crucial that you become a master of your human existence, a master of your energy.

You must become sovereign, in all ways.

You must truly honour and care for all of your bodies so that you are aware of what is your energy and what is not.

It's also important to be able to be aware of your energy and shift it instantaneously back to the high vibrational 5D reality because you can always choose that. It's only when we fall back down into the lower vibrational states that we bang our heads.

Where we are moving into is a beautiful, blissful space where abundance is pouring down on us. It is here for us.

The technologies and the ways of living are abundant and of the energy of love. It is the new earth. It is the new way of life.

Living in The New Wealth is a way of BEing.

You become sovereign when you master how to keep all your bodies high vibrational. It takes work. It takes commitment. It takes time. It takes dedication.

And many people don't make time for this experience of life and are missing out and that is absolutely perfect too. We all have our own journey and no matter where you are on your journey to awakening is perfect.

Just know that you have the choice to say yes to The New Wealth right now.

You have a chance to choose Love, Bliss, Abundance, Peace and Joy in this reality right now. In this exact moment in time. Yes. Now. And Now. And Now. And Now.

You just get to continue to choose Joy and Peace and Bliss and Abundance and Love over and over and over again. Say yes to it. It's here for you.

And when you do… you can become sovereign. Your own sovereignty is to not be dependent on government or handouts in any way.

As the current banking system crumbles, as we bring in artificial intelligence and people's jobs get taken over by the AI, you are going to need a way to survive without a 'time-for-money' job. This is inevitable. This is why you must choose your own sovereignty.

When you tap into this infinite flow of abundance, it's a tap that you don't have to turn off. In other realities right now there are experiences of Divine Abundance. A time and space where you get to do you and live abundantly, and everyone is the vibration of Love. It feels so good.

You may feel it in snippets of time. But what if… what if we all allowed ourselves to be in that experience of flow all the time? That is what happens when you realize that your entire job in life right now is to be a channel for this Divine Currency to flow through you.

That is 'The New Wealth'.

We are a Divine Currency and the more we allow ourselves to tap into that Flow, the more we lean into the discomfort and say yes to the unknown path in front of us, no matter how scary it is, the more we land' The New Wealth.

Keep choosing it. Keep saying yes.

And to become sovereign… learn you.

Learn every aspect of yourself. Take a good, hard look at yourself and realize where you are totally and utterly letting yourself down and choose to stop that.

Take the time to nurture and love on your energetic, mental, spiritual, emotional, and physical selves. Learn the art of keeping each of those bodies clean and clear so that you can live at the highest vibration.

That is what it takes to become Sovereign.

The answer to Magnetism in The New Wealth is to Know Thyself.

We drop into this way of Being in my program 'The Art and Energy of Instant Manifestation'. If you want to begin to embody this way of being, then join me there. You can check out more information about it at https://kerinorley.com/instantmanifestation

Step Three: THE ART AND BALANCE OF CULTIVATING YOUR LIFE-FORCE ENERGY

HOW DO WE CREATE A NEW BALANCE?

We create balance in a few ways. I'm going to talk about 2 of them in here.

YOUR SIX BODIES

This is one important aspect of Creating balance to be magnetic.

I have mentioned your bodies throughout this book already. Here is where we are going to talk a little bit about them so that you can begin to build a relationship with them.

1. Mental Body

Many of you will know this one well. This is your mind, and many people think that manifestation comes from the mind and spend a lot of time cultivating this, but it's not the only way to manifest your desires. If that's all you are doing, it can be quite limiting.

Your mind is currently telling you about all the things you know CONSCIOUSLY. And you may do affirmations or visualization, but if you are not tapping into your unconscious reality, then you are likely still banging your head wondering why you are still in the same place.

Or… you are getting GLIMPSES of it working, but then for days or weeks or months you are shouting at the universe wondering why you're still not there yet.

I TOTALLY GET IT. I did this too! And many of my clients come to me at this point. You are doing the things, but getting haphazard results because you are trying to THINK your way through the process.

In order to shift your reality, you get to look at your multi-dimensional self and work with each aspect, and it will change your life.

So, back to the mental game… you know it. You think empowering thoughts, you shift dis-empowering thoughts. You visualize what you desire in your life. ALL of that can help, just know it's not the only way to bring through your dreams.

2. Physical Body

You know this one too. For me, ever since deepening into my spiritual work, my physical body has felt frustrating and limiting because there is so much more freedom in the other realms.

Our bodies are heavy and dense and can only do certain things. AND… at the same time they are magical and an amazing a tool for manifestation. So make sure that you look after and honour your physical body. It is important.

By the way, Quantum Flow is one of my all time favourite ways to not only move and look after my physical body, but also my other bodies.

It is a movement practice and also a way of life. I share more and more about this with you throughout the book. Please get more info and an experience of Quantum Flow here: www.kerinorley.com/resources

3. Spiritual Body

This is your connection with Spirit, with the Divine. And when you consider that we are all Divine Sparks and we are everything, maybe this will help you deepen into your spiritual self.

If you can even begin to consider that there is more to us than physical matter, then you are heading in the right direction when it comes to building your spiritual relationship with yourself.

Taking time each day to connect with self and spirit will mean that you are giving yourself time to be in a co-creation. In co-creation… you realize that you are NOT in control of what happens to you and yet you know that everything happens FOR YOU.

It's when we don't take time to listen to the signs that are all around us that we get ourselves off our path and bang our heads into walls that we don't have to.

In these moments, take a breath… ask for help… ask for the next aligned step and TRUST that you are being guided down the right path. If you can see it, if you are being given the guidance, trust that it is for you and move forward.

Start small when building this connection. You need to build trust so that when you are asked to do things that scare the living f*ck out of you, you can say yes. You will trust it because you have built the relationship to trust it.

Meditation is a great way to create this relationship. Many people resist meditation. But there are all kinds of ways to meditate. Even riding your bike is a form of meditation. Being in the shower is an awesome space to clear your mind and receive downloads from the Divine. For me, even washing dishes can be a form of meditation.

Ultimately, you are just wanting some time and space to be quiet with yourself and see if you can bring your mind to emptiness and be fully present in the moment. And when those thoughts come in, just notice them. Let them go. Allow yourself to slow your mind down.

Magic happens in the space between the space, when you can have moments of stillness, and some of the most amazing ideas will come to you in that time.

4. Emotional Body

This one... this has been a BIG one for me. I totally ran my life by my emotions, letting them RUN ME for a lot of my life, with many bi-polar tendencies.

In this past year, I have spent a lot of time and energy to shift this pattern: The mood swings that would have me high as a kite and then in the bellows of depression within moments, allowing myself to hide out in a cave for months in depressive states.

It was earlier this year when I finally got to see how much ALLOWING myself to INDULGE in those swings was destroying me and not serving me to create my dreams and share this message with all of you.

Here are 4 ways I am or have supported myself to begin to shift a toxic relationship with my emotional body this past year.

A. Neurofeedback.

It's a total re-wiring of your brain waves. In my brain map, I found out that no matter how much I meditated, breathed, moved, did all the things, my brain did not have the capacity to actually enter into certain states and consequently... my emotions ran the show.

It's not an overnight fix and it is an investment of time and money, but I can HIGHLY recommend that you look into Neurofeedback in your area.

In order to find a qualified practitioner in your area go to

- www.bcia.org > find a practitioner or
- www.eeginfo.com > find a practitioner.

Or you can go to braincodecenters.com for Denver & Dallas area neurofeedback and remote neurofeedback options.

B. Healy.

Another piece that has been a huge part of this transformation in my life in only a small amount of time is my Healy.

Healy is a quantum healing device.

It works your bio-energetic field to see what is out of balance and then you run frequencies to bring you back to balance. It is wicked cool. I wouldn't want to live without one now.

Even during this book writing, my husband is running Healy for me from home because we have only received one of ours so far. It's good and works via distance and even better when you are in close proximity. I'm gonna say it.

So… just get one. Ok? You'll thank me when you have it.

I truly believe that every single BEing on this planet would benefit from having a Healy in their life. It just helps you feel good.

Its job is to raise your vibrations with the click of a button, so all day...it's working for you to clear your field. It's frickin' brilliant!

You can get more info about them here www.kerinorley.com/healy

C. 'Emotional Clearing' and 'The Spiral'.

These tools were a massive part of my transformation. So much so that I became a practitioner to be able to use this tool with my clients.

These tools clear your looping patterns about the way you show up for your emotions and how they run your life.

I do Wealth Alchemy Sessions where we re-wire your field and shift your vibration to align to the wealth you desire to create. They are super powerful.

I also do something called 'The Spiral', which is a very systematic, 1 on 1 experience that goes through all of your chakras and clears your emotional looping, so that by the time we are done with the journey you are done looping on the patterns that have you kept you stuck and stagnant in life.

We go through and clear 22 emotions specifically designed to raise your consciousness. We will clear things like fear, anger, grief, shame, guilt, love, truth, trust, purpose and more.

We don't get rid of the emotions, we will clear the way you show up in those emotions so that you can stop doing the same looping patterns.

It's a transformational journey and changes my clients' lives. It's a true joy and honour to take people through this journey.

If you want to apply for my one on one work, go to webpage: www.kerinorley.com/workwithme and connect with me there.

D. Quantum Flow.

Quantum flow is a movement practice that is more than a movement practice. It's a living, breathing way of life. Quantum Flow was created by my amazing mentor, Juan Pablo Barahona.

In this practice, you use your body to bring through your manifestations by clearing the energy in your physical body. It helps me to manage my emotional state by clearing my field and removing stagnant energy in my body.

It is very strategically put together to connect with your organs, meridians, and so much more. It is a clearing and an activation and movement all in one.

I love this so much and want you to experience the magic of quantum flow, so I have added an experience of this into the resources.

You can check it out for FREE here: https://kerinorley.com/resources.

Come and play and I look forward to hearing about what happens for you as you experience your blissful, natural state of being.

Something you can do right now, is just bring awareness to your emotions. Notice them.

Take time to sit and BE with them instead of eating them down or instead of spending money to make yourself feel better.

Pay attention to how you are feeling. Allow yourself to feel them. And know... Nothing is permanent.

How you feel right now can change in a moment. You are in control of that too. They don't have to control you. If you get angry... notice that you are angry.

Allow yourself to feel angry.

If it's in relation to someone, once you have done your own processing around why you are actually angry, if you feel compelled to speak with them about it, do so in an empowering way.

Then choose another more empowering state. You don't have to stay stuck in anger, depression, frustration, etc., forever. You get to choose.

5. Energetic Body

This is where chakras and meridians come in.

This is the interconnected field of energy that is around our physical body. This energetic field can expand as little or as much as you desire.

We have subtle energetic bodies. The term 'subtle bodies' describes the various layers of vibrating energy that make up a human being beyond the obvious physical layer.

Your energetic body is ultimately your vibration.

This can be a bit more challenging to get your head around if you have never played in the energetic realms before and yet will change your life when you do.

An easy way to explain this is when you walk into a room and you are drawn to a person and you don't know why; it's likely their energy. When you walk into a house or building and get a good feeling about it or a bad feeling about it… it's the energy.

The energy is the unseen but can be felt across the quantum fields.

It's why, if you are diligently working on your mental game and not considering this and banging your head against a wall and wondering why it's not working for you… your energetic field is likely dirty.

It's always vibrating. The question is, is it vibrating high vibes or low vibes?

You can actually measure frequencies. The planet's frequencies are measured with the Schumann resonance. And as we ascend our consciousness the measurements are increasing to record amounts.

David Hawkins created the Scale of Consciousness in his book, 'Power vs Force'. He associates emotions to a vibrational frequency. See how these bodies all play together?

THE NEW WEALTH

When you are in anger, frustration, shame, grief, guilt, fear, and other low vibrational emotions, your energetic field will vibe lower.

When you are in a state of love, bliss, joy, pleasure, peace and other high vibrational states, your energetic field will vibe higher.

This is important because our vibrations attract more of the same vibration.

You can't feel love and fear in the same moment. If you are sending out the vibe of fear, you will get things back to create more fear. Our vibes attract more of the same.

So how do we raise our vibes? One way is to literally shift your emotional state and be in a more high-vibrational state.

To me, one of the best tools I have ever worked with to clear emotional looping is The Spiral. It is absolutely transformational. It's literally designed to clear your way of showing up for many of these supercharged emotions and shift your vibrational field to create magic.

If you are interested in going through the Spiral with me, reach out here: www.kerinorley.com/connectwithme

And, I'll say it again here… Quantum Flow. Yup, in all the ways, you can use Quantum Flow to align your bodies. Remember, you can experience it here: www.kerinorley.com/resources

The energetic system is a massive rabbit hole to dive down. You can study this for years, depending on how deep you want to go.

Diving into the energetic realms has been my obsession for years. You can work with crystals, energetic healers, feng shui, chakras, and more to shift this field.

Even looking at your physical body and seeing if you are putting high quality, high vibrational water and food and superfoods into it so that you are fueling it in a high vibe way. It all adds up.

And... have I mentioned Healy before? Oh yeah... I have. Umm... its whole job is to raise your energetic vibrations with a push of a button. Need I say more?

Get more info here: https://kerinorley.com/Healy

6. Astral Body

For this book... I'm not going to go too far into this, it's an advanced conversation. But you do have an astral body that can travel to other dimensions. And that's all I want to say about that here. ;-) Just focus on these other 5 for now. That will make a big difference for you.

I dive deeper into the 5 bodies and ways to balance them in my course, 'Wealth Codes'. It is a super important concept and way to think about nurturing yourself and creating balance and harmony in your life. This may sound simple, but when you bring into practice what I have said here, magic happens.

Check out Wealth Codes here, if you want to dive into a multi-dimensional way of clearing your field to manifest your dreams. www.kerinorley.com/wealthcodes

THE NEW WEALTH

YOUR DIVINE MASCULINE AND DIVINE FEMININE

This is the second important aspect of creating balance and being magnetic I am going to talk about here.

I started talking about this in the embodiment section already. No matter what sex you are, you have a masculine and feminine energy. And the likelihood that you are in an empowered relationship with either of those aspects of self is slim to none, if you haven't consciously done the work on this already.

In order to bring balance to these aspects of yourself, first bring awareness to it.

Your masculine is driven, wants to take action, is logical and plans things out and wants direction. He is reasoning. He is strong and powerful. He wants to build things.

Your feminine is soft and flowing. She is creative, nurturing and forgiving. She is patient and compassionate and emotional. She is designed to receive.

Again... There are many courses and books designed around this, but this gives you an idea of the traits of the masculine and feminine.

It's highly likely you are leading from one side or the other. I have said for years... You can't only meditate and hope a bag of money will fall on your head and stop there. You need to take the action too.

The masculine and feminine work together in a beautiful balance to help you create your dreams and build your wealth.

The same is said for ACTION... if you are constantly driving but not allowing for the creative flow, then you are limiting yourself in your ability to create magic. It will get to the point of burnout (or maybe it already has and that is why you are reading this book).

There are only so many hours in a day, and so in order to not put more on your plate to hit the next level… it's probably time to take a lot OFF your plate and start to allow yourself into the flow of the feminine and allow yourself to receive magic.

To begin to bring this balance, become aware of where you sit now. Which side of the fence are you on?

If you are too much on the masculine, what would happen if you took time to breathe some more, to walk away from DOING and allow yourself to BE? Take some walks in nature, meditate, dance, paint, find your flow. What works for you?

If you are amazing at being in the feminine, what actions do you know you get to take in order to move you one step closer to your dreams?

Ultimately, I love helping people create a balanced Divine Union between your own masculine and feminine. It's such an empowering journey.

None of this work will happen overnight, but stick with it. It's a lifetime journey. Strap in and go for the ride.

It's worth it and will help you to be able to have more ability to shift your vibration. As you create more balance and harmony by bringing awareness to your masculine and feminine and your multi-dimensional self… you empower yourself to be able to shift your energy to bring through more currency… ultimately, you become more magnetic.

BOOM! Can I get a 'yes, please'?

And YES! This is available for you.

MONEY IS A DANCE

Money is not the piece of paper you hold in your hand. Money is not the numbers on a screen.

Money is a dance. It's a flow. It's a currency. It's an energy.

Money isn't something you hold, it's something that moves through you.

If you want to stay stuck in the 3D level of the world, then continue to look at money as a bunch of numbers.

If you want to transcend that into 'The New Wealth' and a world of Infinite Abundance you must let go of that paradigm and start to move with money. Allow the currency to move through you.

I spoke earlier about living an orgasmic life. This is where that becomes crucial to your ability to call in your dreams right now.

I remember when I realized my orgasmic energy wasn't to be shamed but to be cultivated. That same flow that allows you to relax into orgasm is your life current.

Through movement, through breath, through music, through creative flow, through living a blissful life where you allow yourself to feel pleasure with each and everything you do… you can cultivate that life-force energy.

Your ability to orgasm and bring yourself that pleasure and that freedom is to be in the most intimate, powerful co-creation with the Divine.

And then to take that energy and run it through all day… that is magnetism and it is currency.

But really… as we cross this bridge into the 5D and still fall back into the 3D, or are currently living mostly there and working our way into the space of The New Wealth, we can forget, we can cross timelines and we get in our own way.

We block our flow.

And when we block this flow, when we don't allow for the dance… for the currency to flow through us, we block our capacity to receive Infinite Abundance.

Stop looking to money for the number. The number is only a consequence of your ability to hold energy.

If money is currency and currency is energy, then you get to be in the dance of allowing the currency to FLOW but being able to HOLD the ENERGETIC CONTAINER of that currency to stick around too.

There is an expansion that happens in your energetic field as your wealth increases.

There is an expansion in your energetic field as you expand your tribe, as you stand in your power, as you live your soul-aligned life.

To become sovereign, to be able to dance with Money, this is your work to do.

Your journey is to open yourself up to tap into the currency of Infinite Abundance. I wish I could tell you in a book the way to do this but really, it's a journey. And reading this book is a big part of your journey, right now. For more help navigating the journey as you move forward, join me in one of my programs. You can find more information in the back of the book.

You Are Being Awakened

From here, it's a journey to let go of all the limiting beliefs and stories and darkness and energy in your field that is keeping you trapped into the 3D reality.

It's your journey to cut ties to those limitations and choose to believe in a new way of being, a new way of showing up on this planet. A new way of life.

It's your journey to then choose Love, to choose Peace, to choose Abundance and Bliss.

You get to choose the vibration and currency running through you. There are so many ways to shift this. It may or may not happen overnight, but if you commit to it, it will happen.

This is a journey for a lifetime. There is not ONE THING that will have you dancing with Divine Abundance and allowing it to flow through you. It's many. It's a practice. It's a way of life.

You have the right to choose whichever way you want to go. Truly.

And what you have been deciding in the past is what you are physically looking at in your current reality today.

So ask yourself this… is this reality you are currently experiencing everything you desire in life?

If not… what are you willing to do to walk in the mecca that is ‹The New Wealth'?

What are you committed to doing and how are you committed to BEing, in order to show up for this next level consciousness, this New Wealth?

Choose it now and allow yourself to receive it.

Enjoy the dance with Divine Abundance. Transcend money as numbers. It is so limiting. Do your work to run the currency of Divine Abundance.

If you want to dive deeper into this and understand the mental game behind it, and then clear your energy field to BE this person, check out 'The Art and Energy of Instant Manifestation'.

You will begin to tap into this currency and do this dance and become your own master in the declaration of your Divine Birthright to be Infinitely Abundant.

THE ART OF SURRENDER

This is one of the most challenging pieces for the 3D experience, for the egoic structure to really allow for.

The ego is the part of you that makes you human. It wants to stay where it's at. It wants to stay safe, which is to not change. It's afraid of change. Better the devil it knows.

So the ego's job is to keep you looping in the same patterns and stuck on the same hamster wheel of life.

You get to learn the voice of ego and the voice of truth. Divine Truth. The voice of ego is easier to hear. It's what you know. Even if it's not kind or helpful, it's what you know and that is safe.

To listen to the voice of Divine Truth, that will challenge you. It will ask you to take risks when you are scared out of your mind to do so. It will ask you to say fuck off to fear. It will ask you to dive deep and live a life of courage and walking over and over again into the darkness.

You cannot think your way down this path. You cannot simply mindset your way to the mecca of 'The New Wealth', You cannot think your way to Surrender.

It is when you fully surrender the egoic voice and you collapse the constructs around you that you begin to surrender to the Divine Truth.

Surrender is just that… you give up trying to control your life. You don't. But, you do get to command your life and declare that which you desire becomes yours. When you really get this, your life will change.

You make a decree. You can begin to command your life and declare what you want, but how it shows up for you… there is no control over that, so stop thinking you can.

And it's in this space that you surrender.

It's scary. It will push you out of your comfort zone. You may not like what you are being asked to do, but your commitment to the path and the co-creation is of utmost importance, so you surrender. You let go of thinking you know what is best for you and you follow the Divine Breadcrumbs that are being left for you.

There are signs everywhere, all day long, all around. You will see what you want to see. You will see what is aligned to your beliefs and your physical reality will justify your internal reality. You will prove yourself right. No matter what.

GROUND IT

One of the biggest problems people have in the manifestation piece in teaching and achieving Quantum Manifestation is your ability to GROUND IT.

There are so many of you walking around out there thinking that you can dream about your greatest vision, visualize it, think about it, flimsily talk about it, and maybe even take a couple small steps towards it, and that it will become your reality.

Calling down your dreams is a commitment. It's a process. It's a journey.

And the better you get at getting out of your own way and being 100% committed to the vision, not the current human moment in time, the more you will draw it towards you.

And you must stay the course. Remember that time is not linear.

Quantum leaps happen.

Choose them, believe in them and you can literally be standing in awe that you are in your dreams in what feels like a moment.

Be willing to allow yourself to say yes to bringing those dreams down to earth. Otherwise all you are is a soul with a bunch of dreams while you run around chasing your tail in human form. It doesn't have to be that way.

You get to choose differently, if you want to.

One of the greatest and most important pieces of grounding is to be willing to build a loving relationship with your body and allow it to be the receptor for your dreams to land. This is why I practice Quantum Flow. It's a movement practice designed to help you clear and move the energy in your physical body to bring through your manifestations. It's powerful work.

But you may find it in yoga, weight lifting, running, walking, breathing… wherever and however you connect to your body. Then allow it to be the vessel for bringing down your dreams.

WE ARE ALL AN ENERGETIC TRANSMISSION

We are all energetically coded with a transmission. It's who you are. You don't have to do ANYTHING to be in this transmission. You just get to be you.

And you carry codes that will activate a remembrance in my soul and all the other souls you come across. You see… if we are all the Divine and the Divine is us then we already know everything.

It's just that we chose to forget. When we chose to come to the Earth, to this plane, we chose to forget our Divinity. It is our journey to Remember.

Each person we meet along the way activates something within us. They do it by being in their energy field, in their transmission, in their codes.

Sometimes it takes moments, sometimes years, but when you step into your Divine Purpose you can realize that you don't have to do anything but exist to be abundant and live in a state of love and surrender and allow yourself to receive all that you desire.

We are all coded with a Divine Signature. It's yours and yours only.

And my Purpose, my blueprint, my energetic transmission, is of Magical Source.

So I help people take their dreams and visions from a magical space in the quantum fields and land them here on Earth. I literally am here to help you land your dreams.

It's why so many people come into my field and make more money and create their dreams on every level.

Just by reading this book, by being in my field, you are getting activated with this transmission. You are being coded to Magically bring things down from source energy and have it show up on planet Earth in physical form.

And if you hang with me in a more intimate level, in some of my programs or on my Divine Abundance teams, you will be deeper in this transmission and I will show you ways to empower yourself to bring your dreams into reality.

REVIEW

5 STEPS FOR MAGNETIZING ABUNDANCE

Step 1. Decide what you want.

To DECIDE is to cut off from all other possibilities.

Step 2: Become a master of your 6 Bodies. Become Sovereign.

Own your own space and know what is yours and what is others. Take Radical Responsibility.

Step 3: The art and balance of cultivating your Life-force energy.

Move your energy to become magnetic. Cultivate your energy within and let it run through you. Shine.

Step 4: Surrender.

Let go of thinking you can control anything in your life. All you can do is decide the end goal and then realize you have no idea how it will show up, just that it will, and surrender. Surrender. Surrender.

Please be clear… surrender does NOT mean be a victim. It is NOT giving your power away. It is NOT throwing in the towel and being pissed that life didn't show up for you.

Surrender IS walking the path in co-creation with the Divine, which is you and taking aligned ACTIONS. So walking your true soul's path.

Step 5: Ground it. Bring it down to Earth.

Sit on the earth. Eat grounding foods. Be in your body and ground your dreams into reality. Take the actions! Remember this step. ;-)

ACTIVATION QUESTIONS:

Questions to ponder for yourself or to discuss at a book club.

1. What are your 2 top takeaways around magnetizing abundance from this section that if you were to embody them, if you were to implement them into your life, would allow you to shift closer to your dreams?

2. What got triggered in you as you read this? What can you do to be with that trigger and love it?

3. What activated within you around magnetizing abundance and growing your wealth? Where do you feel you have woken up and remembered something? Where is there a new spark of light guiding you?

4. What is that spark guiding you towards?

5. Which of your 5 bodies would you like to focus on building a relationship with right now?

6. Are you more masculine or feminine dominant? What are you going to do to cultivate your relationships with the masculine and feminine?

7. What are you ABSOLUTELY committed to creating now? Write it out. Over and over again. Breathe it in, feel it, BE it. DECIDE right now that it is yours.

SECTION 5
HOLDING YOUR WEALTH

I could title this section, 'Just because you have it, doesn't mean you have to spend it.'

I could end it there too. Because ultimately that is how you hold wealth. The secret's out.

Don't spend it all.

But many of you have so many totally unhelpful and disempowering beliefs about money and wealth and what it means, and you completely block yourself from allowing yourself to hold onto your wealth.

And instead, no matter how much you make, no matter how hard you work, you are still basically living paycheck to paycheck and wondering how you will pay your bills, with nothing behind you to help you, in case of a rainy day.

You haven't learned that you have to allow yourself to energetically expand your container to hold onto wealth.

It is a massive expansion of energy with the more currency you allow yourself to pool around you. And you have to choose to let go of all your disempowering stories and trust that there is another way to live life and keep saying yes to it.

You get to do the inner and outer work that will keep your energetic field clear to allow the energy of holding that money.

THE NEW WEALTH

This is how generational wealth gets squandered. The generation who makes it has to expand their energy field to be able to hold it in the first place.

The second generation may or may not lose it depending on what values and beliefs actually got passed onto them around wealth. If it makes it to the third generation... many were given everything. And because of privilege, we kind of expect that it will be there, but that's not true for many.

We, in the third generation of wealth, have to figure out how to hold the energetic container for wealth in a way that is aligned to us, without the same guidance and mentorship we learned from the first generation.

It's a big part of the work I want to bring to this planet. Helping people to hold onto generational wealth. There are energetic reasons it gets squandered and it doesn't have to be this way.

Remember, this piece right here is the whole reason that I do everything I do in my life. I will not be one of the 3rd generational family legacy wealth that just throws it away. No thank you.

And so it has been a MISSION to figure out why family legacy wealth rarely lasts past the third generation and how to shift this paradigm. Mostly for purely selfish reasons. I didn't want to frivolously spend all the money that has been passed on to me. I want to carry on the legacy my grandparents have left in all the ways. Hence writing this book.

It's not taught anywhere that I have seen... how to hold onto generational wealth from an energetic, mental, emotional and spiritual perspective. I have looked for it. So, I have an online group program to help people hold onto wealth and I work with people one on one, in this situation, who want to expand their wealth.

This program is for you if:

- You have been born into generational wealth;
- You have been divorced and have not had to have the financial responsibility and you get a lump sum of money in a settlement; or
- You are a growing entrepreneur that is getting 5-figure plus months and you are making more money than ever before but can't figure out why you are still living paycheck to paycheck with nothing to show for all the work and growth, financially.

But the same principles apply if you are not any of those people and you want to start to hold your wealth, no matter what.

WHAT ARE THE PRINCIPLES TO APPLY TO EXPAND YOUR CONTAINER TO HOLD WEALTH?

As always... first things first.

Step One: Decide You Want To.

You won't do anything you don't decide to do. You must cut off from all other possibilities.

Cut off from living paycheck to paycheck with nothing behind you, or leave living with only a few weeks' worth of bills getting paid behind you.

Just declare that you no longer desire that. Continually choose that your wealth is growing. Continually choose that you easily have money left over to save.

Decide that your bank account is constantly growing and that you are accumulating more and more money, or more and more currency, and keep choosing it. Allow it to flow to you.

You are worthy of being abundantly wealthy.

This is available for all of you that are reading this. If you have drawn this into your field, you are ready for quantum leaps. As wild as this may sound. It's the truth.

Step one: Decide you want it.

Step Two: Choose It.

If you don't back up the decision with action, you haven't actually decided. If you want this manifestation of an accumulation of financial wealth in your field, you have to land it on planet Earth. You have to make it physical. You must take action towards it.

It seems so logical but many of you are paralyzed in fear and don't move towards your dreams. You keep yourself BUSY, sure. But that is not necessarily moving the needle closer to your dreams. As often proven by making more and more money and having nothing extra to show for it.

Or even in doing something you think you 'SHOULD' be doing but really you are just moving through life, knowing there is something more fulfilling out there for you. Catch my drift?

And remember, The New Wealth is a currency. And you get to be amazing with your personal practices to be able to have the space to bring through this currency and hold it. So if you are not in a full fuck-yes, soul-aligned life, then you are limiting yourself in your Divine Connection and this Infinite Abundance.

We are going to keep coming back to this, because I want you to truly understand how important these principles are for your life. And to have something land, you really get to see it multiple ways, so I'm showing you. Ok? Listen up.

You are multi-dimensional so care for your multi-dimensional self and you will be able to expand your container to hold your wealth in 'The New Wealth'.

This Infinite Abundance is available for all of us.

Step two, choose it. In every action of your day, choose this version. Keep choosing the new decision and allow yourself to see it and receive it.

THE NEW WEALTH

Remember, what you look for, you will see. ;-)

Actions to take as you choose it:

1. Set yourself up physically to hold money. Look into what is the best way to hold it on this earth plane.
   Will you use a separate savings account with a small interest in it? Maybe a CD? This will force you to hold it, because you don't get the interest if you take it out pre-term. ;-)

   Or you can look into DeFi and have your money working for you making at least 8% compounding interest.

   Check out this interview with Rossco Paddison to find out more about Decentralized Finance. Think a banking system outside of our current corrupt banking system.

   www.kerinorley.com/resources

2. You will want to start looking for a financial team, if you don't already have them. You will want an accountant who is aligned in thought with you. Depending on your situation, if you don't already have one, it is a good idea to look for a financial advisor, of course taking into consideration your futuristic thought in investing.

   Meaning, don't talk to an old guy who doesn't know anything about digital currency. You will get a very limited perspective.

   Do talk to a person who is educated in all ways of investing right now from real estate, cryptocurrency, stock market, DeFi and more.

3. And of course, by the end of this book, I will have shown you a new way of doing money on this planet. We have a new template being formed for ways for us to transact in

the 3D but have growth from compounding interest for us, the people, not the banks.

So, there is that and you may want to incorporate learning about having this work for you too. If consistent 7.5-8.5% compounding interest or expanding your wealth through digital currency intrigues you then get more info here: www.kerinorley.com/resources.

Step Three: Do Whatever It Takes To Shift Your Vibration and Raise It to That Of Love, Joy, Bliss, Abundance and Peace.

It's not going to happen overnight. You have a lifetime, even lifetimes, of limiting stories and loops to unwind.

Unless you have been doing the quantum clearing work, you likely have dark and heavy density in your field that is keeping you weighed down and stuck in the reality of lack and limitation.

Stuck in the 3D reality.

Commit to whatever it takes for as long as it takes to shift this.

Over the years, you will work with multiple practitioners, you will use different modalities, you will have many egoic deaths, you will clear shadow, you will learn about fueling your body with high vibrational foods, you will learn ways to move energy through your body, you will discover how to surrender into the trance of the other realms, you will require having healing devices like Healy and more to do ALL THE THINGS.

PS- If you don't know what Healy is, you gotta check it out here www.kerinorley.com/healy.

It's a magical device that reads your quantum fields and will shift your vibration according to what is most relevant to you in the moment.

I believe every home in the world would benefit from this device and it will raise the consciousness of the planet by helping all of us live a higher vibrational life with so much ease.

Step 3: Do the work to raise your vibes.

Step Four: Say Yes.

Allow yourself to receive the Infinite Abundance and say yes to HOLDING some, even if it's only $1/week to start with, just start building your nest egg.

As you start to feel comfortable putting a certain amount aside, increase that. Your energetic field can withstand increases by 10% every 3 months. It's enough time for it to become your normal.

You do not have to understand HOW it will happen, just trust that it will and look for it. Allow yourself to receive it. It wants to flow to you and through you.

Step 4: Say yes.

THE FOUR STEPS TO EXPAND YOUR CONTAINER TO HOLD WEALTH

1. Decide.
2. Choose it.
   2a. Take the aligned actions.
3. Do whatever it takes to shift your vibration to that of Love, Abundance, Joy, Bliss and Peace.
4. Say yes.

EMBODIMENT PRACTICES FOR HOLDING YOUR WEALTH

Well if wealth is a currency, then you get to learn how to move this currency. In the 'The New Wealth', you use all your bodies as an antenna to bring through your manifestations. So if that is the case… you get to learn how to be a channel for Infinite Abundance.

When you choose to open up your channel for this, embodiment practices are critical. At the end of the day… you are embodying a vision into the 3D reality. It already exists in another reality, now you have to ground it down into this plane. And the thing that keeps you in this plane is your physical body.

So when we talk about embodiment practices, we are talking about ways to bring your vision into your 3D field. It is to bring it through your body to land on this earth right now.

So in order to do this, you get to make a commitment to yourself that you will look after all of your bodies.

Here are examples of embodiment practices (in no particular order):

Quantum Flow

This practice will change your life if you actually use it and embody the Quantum Flow Lifestyle. You see, creating flow states isn't just about visualizing and meditating… there is also clearing your field and your body and being a clear channel.

In order to do this, you get to BE the person who chooses this lifestyle and does your practices so that you land your dreams like magic.

To experience Quantum Flow, please go and check out this bonus video here: https://kerinorley.com/resources

Dance

Move your body. Let it move you. Find the sticky spots. Breathe into it. Explore outside your comfort zone, the edges of where your body wants to go. It will open up your expansion off the dance floor too.

Use dance to move stuck and stagnant energy and to connect with your body and soul. The key to this is to find music that lifts you up and allow yourself to totally let go and let your body move you.

Self-pleasure

Ahhh… one of the most magical ways to embody and connect to your dreams. The moment of orgasm is the point of creation.

You get to have orgasmic co-creation with the Divine, which is of course, you. And in that moment… you send orgasmic ripples into the field calling in your desires.

Yes please?!

For many of my clients, this is a new concept and can throw people a bit out of whack for a second. So give yourself a moment to take this in. It's all good. Whatever you do, just don't shy away from the power of this practice.

There is so much shame in the collective about self-pleasure. Also, as women, we are often deemed sluts if we allow ourselves to receive pleasure whilst men are hailed for it, hey? Doesn't even make sense. But that is what is in the collective about sexual energy and pleasure.

So, please be willing to put that down, forever. Well, at least long enough to try this out. To allow yourself to explore yourself for pleasure. As you do, if you begin to fully surrender, your magnetism will ignite.

By the way, you are not a sinner. You are not a bad person for giving yourself pleasure. In fact, you are a magical person when you do, and fully surrender into the co-creation and create sparks of magic. BOOM!

Intimacy OR In to me I see

'In to me I see' – Let's take it from that perspective.

Being intimate with someone is ultimately letting you and the other person see you at the core of who you are.

This is different from self-pleasure. Intimacy can be sexual with your partner. It can come from your partner without sex, too.

Intimacy can come from mutual friends also. You can love other beings and also love your partner.

Intimacy can come in conversations or hugs or dancing together, it can come in many ways. When you allow yourself to be intimate with other BEings, your heart will crack open and you vibrate at LOVE.

Remember, 'The New Wealth' is the vibration of love. ;-)

Are you catching on yet? Your journey right now is to do whatever it takes to clear your stuff so that you can

radiate at the vibration of Love? What a wonderful way to BE, hey?

Say yes to it.

Food

Choose nourishing, whole foods that will create energy and vitality in your system versus energy that weighs you down and clogs your system.

Look at your body as an amazing machine for manifestation and keep it running in the most optimal way. And then, eat and pay attention to which foods feel heavy or give you gas or have you feeling sleepy, etc. Build a relationship with your body and food so that you are always giving it what it wants and asks for.

This one has been the hardest for me, personally. Overcoming addiction to food has been a tough one for me. I empathize. I am choosing to nourish my body and I am learning to listen to it. All we can do is do our best in each moment of time.

That said, my suggestion for you in regards to food is; FUCK THE RULES. They don't work. UGH! They just make you feel worse when you don't fully comply with every mouthful.

Focus on whole foods. Listen to your body. Eat protein, good fats, vegetables and fruit. Stick to eating that as much as possible.

Give yourself full permission to eat whatever your body *really* asks for. Learn to listen to your body, not your ego or your shadow or the void that you are filling so that you don't have to feel or pay attention to the pain within.

The truth is... Your body wants to be nourished and if you move beyond the noise in your mind, it will choose beautiful, nourishing foods that come from the earth to eat.

Writing

Journaling is a great way to mentally bring things down to the planet.

Many people look at journaling and think... Ugh! I don't want to write. Or you learned to journal in a way that was uninspiring, like sitting and writing about your day. Boring. You already lived it, right?

Journaling is a wonderful way to get clear about your dreams and to write your future into reality.

I love teaching journaling practices and opening this doorway for my clients. It's so powerful. The best place for you to start, if you don't have a journaling practice already, is to start writing out what you desire in life, in all areas.

Dive deep. Allow yourself to dream and get into the details.

Write about where you want to be living, who is around you, the way you are treated, the way you treat yourself, what you eat, how you look, how you move, what results you are creating, how you magnetize your clients to you, how you grow your wealth, how much money you have saved, etc.

Write your dreams into reality. Remembering... what you focus on is what you get. Take some time to allow yourself to dream and then *take the actions* towards those goals.

THE NEW WEALTH

People often ask me, 'Do I have to handwrite this?' My answer is, 'You can do it any way you want.' You are the creator of your own reality. And, it's said that when we use the motion to put pen to paper, it wires into our brains in a way that it doesn't by typing or speaking.

Personally… my creation journaling is done in a beautiful journal that makes me feel good, with a pen that writes with ease and flow and I love the way it feels.

I recommend that for you, and you always get to do you. If you have resistance to it, I suggest you just give it a go.

Breakthrough the resistance and see what happens as you do.

There are more embodiment tools that I do with my clients, but this will get you started with some tools to call down your dreams from the ethers.

And of course, as you call it down and bring this energy with you, remember to allow yourself to HOLD ONTO IT. ;-)

DANCE WITH MONEY PART 2

I talked about dancing with money in the Magnetizing Abundance section and I want to bring it up again here too, because the dance continues as you discover how to HOLD money.

When I talk about holding onto money, it is an interesting dance because at the end of the day… it's currency and we want it FLOWING. Right?

So how do we hold it and flow at the same time? THAT is the dance.

It's NOT an either/or. It's an AND. So it's not I either have it flow through me OR I hold onto every penny. It's the currency of 'money' flows through me AND I get to keep some too.

A really good example of this is thinking about a river.

A running river has flow, current, movement. And in this river, there will be pockets of water called eddies. In the eddies, water swirls around in this vortex and hangs in that vortex all whilst other water flows right on by.

The river has ways of flowing and holding at the same time.

This is how you get to dance with money.

In your reality, this will look something like this…

You have to get real about where you are at financially. And then create a plan.

THE NEW WEALTH

For now, it may mean setting up a basic savings account where you put money aside each week or month to grow your savings. It may start with $5/week or month, if that's all that feels safe. And if that's it, celebrate that you are starting.

You may know that you can afford much more than that and you challenge yourself to watch your spending and choose to really begin to create a safety net for yourself and make it your priority for your money versus frivolously spending. This can happen with so much ease if you start to look at your spending.

I don't know one person I have spoken to about this that hasn't had somewhere they can pull back on spending and not miss it, so that they can start focusing on holding their wealth.

We, as a society, have it shown to us by the governments printing trillions of dollars on demand and creating more debt than many of us can even wrap our heads around, that whenever we need or desire more money, we can access it via credit. And, we live in a consumer-based society that drills into you that more is better.

Put those things together and many of you reading this are probably over-spending on things that don't actually serve you.

Just like using food to fill a void and over-eating... we as humans can use shopping and spending money to fill a void that ultimately doesn't get filled, and so we spend more and more and more, instead of valuing ourselves enough to STOP THAT and give ourselves the space to HOLD onto our money.

This is a powerful and important piece right here.

Generally speaking, your ability to hold onto your money (currency) is an energetic experience and if you are not able to, it's an energetic leak. Your mind, your emotions, your energy are all telling you that you can't on some unconscious level.

Here are some beliefs that I hear a lot that can create patterns of letting money flow right through you…

- Money is bad.
- Money is the root of all evil.
- Rich people are ass holes.
- Relationships will fall apart if I have money.
- I will have to pay more taxes and I don't want to support a government that I don't believe in.
- I am not responsible enough to have that money.
- I don't know what to do with money.
- It's okay. I like living a frugal life.
- I don't NEED anything more.
- Money causes war.
- I don't want my family and friends to take advantage of me.
- Add yours here. There are tons more that you can be carrying.

Can you see how, if you are carrying any of these beliefs, you will turn away money from showing up but also from holding onto it if you do have some. It's because, inherently, you believe that having money will bring you problems or pain, so you unconsciously sabotage yourself and then it flows right through you. UGH!

I will say it again and again and again throughout this book… If you want to shift these patterns, you are going to have to look at these unconscious ways of sabotaging yourself and clear your field and then CHOOSE TO DO IT DIFFERENTLY.

None of this will change, as if by magic, unless you DECIDE that it will and take the aligned actions to make the changes.

THE NEW WEALTH

In this situation… that may look like this…

1. You DECIDE that you are going to take a look at your money situation.

2. You look at all your spending. And you look at what you are making. Are you over or under-spending?

3. You decide what you want to have put aside.
   A good start is having enough money so that you can live for at least 3 months without working. That will feel so amazing to have, if you don't have it already. If you have this already… can you stretch yourself further?

   Where money has a direction to go, it will flow. So… if you want to increase your savings/investing then put more money aside for it and money will FLOW to you for that.

4. Figure out how much you can put aside to create that nest egg and then do it. Don't let emotion get involved. Set it up as an automated payment to a separate account and watch it grow. Make it a game. Have fun with it.

5. This is NOT punishment. This is not meant to be so limiting that you don't enjoy life. AND… there are sacrifices that will likely be made. Get excited for that because the feeling of knowing that you are not going to end up on the streets if you don't make money this week is AMAZING and worth any small sacrifices.

   Those sacrifices may be to drink less alcohol or less takeaway coffee. Saving yourself $5–$20 a day or more for some of you. What if you had less of it? Maybe you would even feel more alive and vibrant too AND be saving money.

Just look around... There are always places we can choose to not spend our money instead of frivolously spending it to fill a void.

Also... look at that void you are filling. This work is some of the deeper work I do with my clients; to really dive in and look at your patterns around money and wealth and clear them from your field so they are not a problem for you and not driving you anymore.

We all have looping patterns that keep us stuck and trapped in patterns that don't serve us. Ultimately, unless you have done the inner work to shift this, you are still running around looping with emotional triggers from your first 7 years of life playing on repeat and they DO NOT serve you.

And here is where I see a problem with MANY people. You think you can change it all on your own.

6. You think you can see these patterns and clear them from your field without any help.

If you could see all your shadow spots on your own, they wouldn't be in the shadow. You get to have someone to support you to bring awareness to where you are blocking yourself.

Another thing...

7. You may be thinking, 'I have worked with one person or maybe more to shift my money story and it didn't really work, so why keep going?'

Let me tell you, it does not matter what level of life you are playing at. It does not matter how much money you have or don't have. It does not matter what your background is and how you were raised… You have these deep-seated patterns that are 100% running your life.

The real work is to have awareness around these and then do whatever it takes to make sure that they are not running your life anymore.

The work I do with my clients is to help find these unconscious loops and clear them, so they are no longer how you drive your life. I take people through emotional clearing work and quantum clearing work that will shift these patterns in the quantum fields, and your life will not be the same again.

Within months of working with me…

- One client came in and wanted to build her team. She's in the financial industry, already making multi-6-figures in her business and was great at bringing her own clients on, but she knew that she would have more impact and her income would also grow if she worked to help other people come on-board to make a business of financial advising too.

  In the past 8 months since our work has started together, she has brought on 24 NEW agents, who are bringing on new clients and helping more people and more are coming. Nice team growth there, if you ask me. ;-)

  When she journeyed through The Art and Energy of Instant Manifestation, she set a big stretchy goal to hit $100,000 in that 7 weeks not knowing how that would happen and she did it.

- I have a client that has gone from broke and needing to borrow money to landing a job contract of over $250,000 when commissions are included and then committed to growing his wealth portfolio in big ways so that he has financial security.

- One client was online not making any money sharing her message for a year, and we started working together, and she has brought on new clients for a group, for individual work, and is now taking off growing her Healy business with me. The flow has been uncorked and she's finally able to be financially rewarded for her amazing work in the world.

- One client already has a 7-figure business and she increased her profit by 10% last year.
More importantly… our work together has allowed her to step into MAGIC and her FEMININE. Meaning that she is in more flow. She is allowing herself to RECEIVE.

And whilst she made more money, some of the biggest impact our work has had for her was in relation to her husband.

They were on the way to moving out and divorce when our work started… like she was looking at apartments the day that we first met… and that didn't happen, and their relationship has improved greatly.

Relationship shifts happen A LOT working with me. People either fall more in love or realize you are not in alignment with the person and you finally have the courage to walk away. Either way is perfect. ;-)

If this feels like you, for both men and women, you know that you have the drive to do anything. You have the ability to make things happen. And at some point, you realize that it's hard, you are pushing things up a hill and there are only so many hours in a day and only one of you. So if you want your next-level vision to become your reality, there is a fear around HOW and BURNOUT.

It's because you are trying to grow your wealth in a purely masculine way.

When we clear your stuff around money, when we clear your stuff around your emotional triggers that are running your life right now… MAGIC HAPPENS.

None of my clients are working 'harder' or 'differently' than before. They are doing the work to move past these blocks and limitations that have been running them for years and allowing for flow and magic.

At the end of this book, I will share the ways that you can work with me. If you know you are ready to clear your limitations around magnetizing, holding and growing your wealth, then be sure to check that out and see what feels aligned for you. I would love to support you in growing your wealth!

SURRENDER INTO GROWTH

I talked about surrender in the aspect of magnetizing your wealth. Now let's talk about it in the aspect of HOLDING your wealth.

It's a fine line to run here. I was taught my whole life to manage lump sums of money and to save for a rainy day.

When I was 14, I was given $500 in a checking account and that was my allowance for the year. I could spend it all in one place or I could make it last for the year.

At the time, I also worked for my mom at her gourmet food store. It was about the only way I could see her, because she was always there. But it worked. I hung with her and did work around the store and she paid me. So I always had money saved behind me and would spend what I earned. This habit started back then.

I don't remember a time in my life when I didn't have savings. My kids are the same way.

People tend to think that when you grow up in wealth you never have to work for anything. On the contrary, I was taught to work for it all. Because truthfully… Empires are not made overnight and you have to work a lot to get there.

And for some crazy reason, people think that you can sit on your butt and work a few hours a week to build yourself to the place that you have the LUXURY of living off of your passive income.

I'm gonna bust this myth right here.

People come to me ALL THE TIME with the *belief they want to bust through of* … *'I have to work hard to make money.'*

And you think it's what holds you back.

THE NEW WEALTH

There is an ASPECT of that which is true. But it's not really the aspect you are thinking of.

You want to be done working tireless hours in the hopes that one day you will not be chasing your tail financially. And you think that because you were drilled that you have to work hard for your money that that is a limiting belief.

The thing is that at some level, you do have to work for it. I'm sharing this to say to you that many people think that when you are born into money that everything is handed to you on a silver platter.

Whilst some of that is definitely true, I also learned to work for my keep. And I learned this because in order for my grandparents to build the legacy they did, they worked for it. The whole family worked for it. All of the 2nd generation worked in the family business at some point in time.

Not all families teach the next generation to earn their keep, but my family most certainly did. And I learned that you have to work for your money.

Now, here is the distinction that will make the biggest difference for you.

Instead of working tirelessly at a job that you hate that is not aligned with your purpose, or instead of running a business that drains you and doesn't bring you joy…

Work at what you love.

And work SMARTER.

My grandparents worked a lot. The difference is that they leveraged their time and energy. To get into the full teaching around this is for another time, but for this purpose, understand that distinction of the belief around working hard.

If you want your dreams, you are going to have to work for it. But when you are doing your soul-aligned work, you WANT TO DO THE WORK.

I would want to explode if I wasn't bringing this work to the world, and I would probably shrivel up and die.

That's my truth around purpose work.

It is that important.

My life is my work, including play, self-care, relaxing and fun. It's all a big jumble together. I love sharing this message with you and helping raise people up to a higher vibration and a more abundant way of living. It brings me an immense amount of joy.

And…locking yourself away for a week to write a book is WORK. Please don't mistake this. But I am LOVING this experience and all the 'stuff' it brings with it (and there is a lot of that).

You may work harder than you have ever worked before in your life to achieve your dreams, but the intention is that you love every step of the way. Even the most challenging ones.

And that wherever possible, you work smarter. You look for ways to leverage yourself.

And of course this does not mean that you have to work 80 hour weeks with no rest. But please realize working and doing stuff you may not want to do so that you get the job done is part of the journey to success.

So what does this have to do with surrender?

Surrender your life to the greater cause. Surrender the thought that you can sit on your butt and do nothing and hope that you will get rich.

THE NEW WEALTH

Allow yourself to do the thing that your heart and soul desires the most, and surrender into everything that comes with that.

And, surrender your limitations, your beliefs, your negative thinking and energy so that you can rise above it. Whatever is no longer serving you, let it go.

The surrender piece is the hardest when you truly let go and have to trust, because you don't necessarily know HOW you will amass your wealth. You just get to trust that by making the decision, setting the intention and taking the aligned actions, one day you will have the wealth you deeply desire.

As we call down this New Wealth, we get to surrender into the unknown of that too. We have ways to do this in the 3D reality right now, but things will evolve and change, for sure, in the coming years. And it's up to all of us to let go of thinking we know, because we don't.

We are in a time of great transformation and what has worked in the past will not necessarily work in the energy moving forward.

We are in unprecedented times, so best to let go of thinking you can control anything about what is happening right now. You can't, and there are powers and forces greater than us that are at work right now to shift the energy of this planet.

Surrender to the ride and keep choosing your desires.

Keep taking aligned actions towards them and trust with every cell of your being that what you are dreaming about is absolutely possible, even if you have no idea how it will happen.

That is the game of surrender.

REVIEW

The Four Steps To Expand Your Container To Hold Wealth

1. Decide.
2. Choose it.
   2a. Take the aligned actions.
3. Do whatever it takes to shift your vibration to that of Love, Abundance, Joy, Bliss and Peace.
4. Say yes.

Ideas of Embodiment Practices for Holding Your Wealth:

1. Quantum Flow
Experience it in this Bonus video: www.kerinorley.com/resources
2. Dance
3. Self-Pleasure
4. Intimacy
5. Food
6. Writing/Journaling

Dance With Money

Build a relationship with money that allows you to hold onto it whilst not clinging so hard that you stop the flow.

Remember, it's currency. It wants to flow. Give it a place to go.

Surrender Into Growth

Be willing to do the work and take the ALIGNED actions without needing to control it all.

THE NEW WEALTH

> Let go of the unhelpful thoughts that are stopping you from creating your dreams and say yes. Continue to say yes every single day to what you desire and allow it to show up for you. You don't need to know how. I know it can be tough to get your mind around this, but this is super important.
>
> You cannot control what happens to bring your dreams your way. You can surrender and get really amazing at commanding what you want and going with the flow, knowing that everything is always working FOR you, even the ickier parts of life… it's all happening FOR you.

ACTIVATION QUESTIONS:

1. What are your 2 top takeaways from this section that – if you were to embody them and implement them into your life – would allow you to shift closer to your dreams?

2. What activated within you around holding your wealth? Where do you feel you have woken up and remembered something? Where is there a new spark of light guiding you?

3. What is that spark guiding you towards?

4. Which embodiment practice(s) are you drawn towards? Where can you include them in your life? When in your schedule are you committed to doing the practice(s)?

5. Ask yourself: Where do I feel stuck in my dance with money? What is available for me right now to allow me to create even more flow?

6. Another question to write/journal about: What are the things I get to let go of that I am most scared to, or just don't want to, that if I did, I would be standing in my dreams? Write a list. Keep writing through the pauses until you have dumped them all.

After you have finished writing those out… write a list of what you can do instead of the unhelpful behavior, and put your focus on doing those things instead. #surrender

And one more journaling prompt to help rewire yourself to Surrender.

The reason this is powerful is because what you believe and EXPECT to be normal is what happens for you. So, for 2 journaling pages finish this sentence…

THE NEW WEALTH

No matter what I do…

Examples:

- No matter what I do, money flows to me and I am always looked after abundantly.
- No matter what I do, I always have money left over every month.
- No matter what I do, I always know the next, right-aligned action to take.
- No matter what I do, my tribe grows.
- No matter what I do, I always pay my bills on time.
- No matter what I do, I feel healthy and vibrant.
- Etc., etc.

Don't get stuck in the mind about this. You get to make up your reality. This will help your belief system to align to, "It doesn't matter what I do, I get to have my dreams here."

The reality is… there are multiple ways to get to your destination… so SURRENDER and trust you are always wherever you are meant to be, and that life is happening FOR you, because you decided that No Matter What… it gets to.

SECTION 6
LEAVE YOUR LEGACY

WHAT IS A LEGACY?

The etymology of legacy according to https://www.etymonline.com/word/legacy is:

late 14c., *legacie*, "body of persons sent on a mission," from Medieval Latin *legatia*, from Latin *legatus* "ambassador, envoy, deputy," noun use of past participle of *legare* "send with a commission, appoint as deputy, appoint by a last will" (see legate). Sense of "property left by will, a gift by will" appeared in Scottish mid-15c. *Legacy-hunter* is attested from 1690s. French *legs* "a legacy" is a bad spelling of Old French *lais* (see lease (n.)). French *legacie* is attested only from 16c.

So according to its origins, summed up… legacy is to be sent on a mission, to be appointed by last will or is a sense of property left by will.

What if we turned that into… we are all on a Divine mission from source? Our souls are here with a Divine Purpose and what you are leaving 'by will' is your impact, your energetic blueprint on this planet. What if your legacy is whether or not you chose love or fear?

What if we thought about legacy like that?

THE NEW WEALTH

We ALL have the opportunity to leave a legacy on this planet, to leave our own energetic blueprint. And the truth of it is… you are leaving a legacy, whether it's a negative or positive impact on the planet, and it is up to each individual on the planet to decide the blueprint they will leave.

And, even if you are not the person who has written or will write a book or have a business as your legacy, that's all good. You have other ways to leave your mark.

My children are my greatest legacy to this planet, by far. No matter how far and wide my impact spreads. Even as it touches millions of lives, my greatest legacy will be my beautiful boys.

NEVER get discouraged that you are only one person. My grandmother was only one person, too, and she had one massive impact on this planet. My grandfather was only one person and my goodness did he create waves on this planet.

When my grandmother passed away and we came together as a family to mourn her loss, we spoke to the rabbi for hours the night before the funeral so that she could share stories from the family at the funeral.

I sat there in awe listening to the stories each of us told. My grandma was blessed with a beautiful life and left a legacy that has touched millions of people around the world.

She was an advocate for inner-city kids to get out into nature and experience walking through the woods, and so she helped create a program in the Chicago Public Schools to get kids out of the city for a weekend.

She was an advocate for the Jewish faith. There is a day camp in both her and my grandfather's name for Jewish kids to go to.

Both of my grandparents were major contributors to Jewish organisations and to our synagogue, because it was such an important part of their faith and world.

She was the first female president to sit on the Jewish Community Centre Board of Chicago in 1968.

She was involved in environmental organisations and in medical support and I'm sure many others.

Over the years my grandparents gave away 10s of millions of dollars to causes that were close to their heart. Not only did they give their money, they often gave their time and energy.

I'm saying this to say, my grandparents left a massive legacy. Not just one that has made my life even more abundant, but has touched millions of lives for generations to come.

And, honestly, what I can say from my heart, her greatest, most prized legacy to the world was all of us. Her family was her pride and joy and she reigned over her family like the Empress she was. And yes, we literally called my grandma 'The Empress'. Reign as 'The Empress' she did in the most elegant way, usually getting what she wanted.

I learned to be an Empress from one the best Empresses this world has ever seen.

This is one of my favorite pictures of my gram. I think she looks like the most elegant woman here, truly embodying her Empress.

THE NEW WEALTH

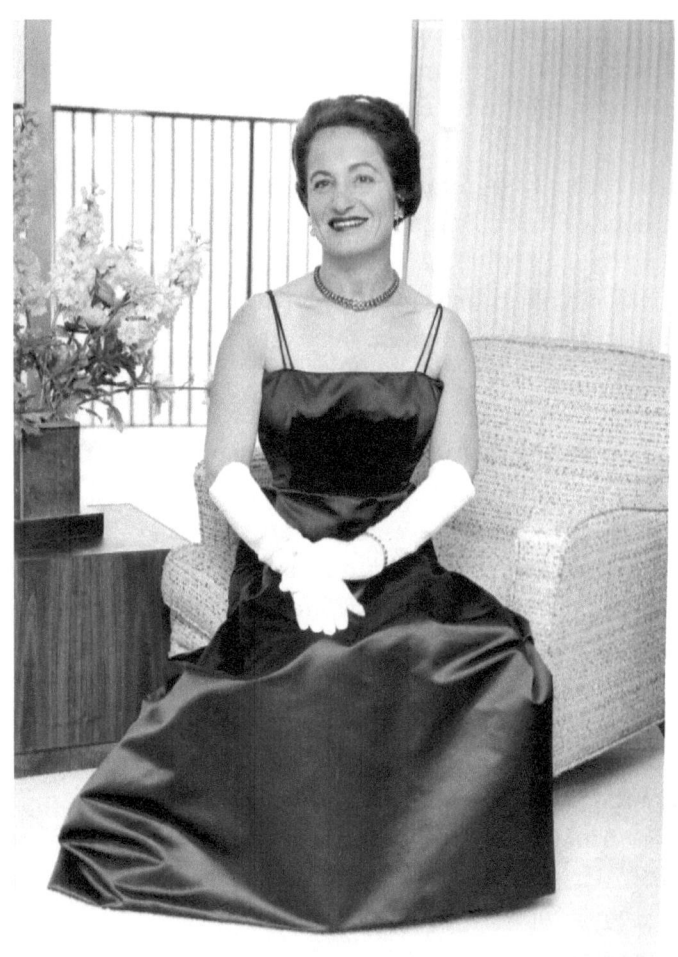

THE WAY I SEE IT THERE ARE FOUR TYPES OF LEGACY

1. Energetic Legacy

A. This is your energetic blueprint. This is what energy you bring to this planet. This is what consciousness you choose to exist in. This is the energetic transmission that each and every one of us carries.

B. This is also your ability to leave a legacy in the time and energy that you give.

Think Mother Theresa.

She had a massive impact on the planet and her legacy had nothing to do with her own financial wealth and everything to do with her time and energy and dedication to a cause.

Mother Theresa Complex - Martyrdom Wake Up Call.

Here is where you have to be mindful of the Mother Theresa complex. I see this in the spiritual community all the time and I say this with love…

You give and give when financially you, yourself, are not full. It's way more challenging to give from a cup that is not full. And you think that by doing so you will be deemed more worthy of your dreams becoming your reality because you did it so frugally.

I'm by no means judging anyone for the way they choose to live their life. I, too, have pinched pennies, wondered where rent money is coming from, woken at night in fear around where the money will come from? Yeah… I've been there, done that

THE NEW WEALTH

too. I get that I have done it from a more privileged place. I do not deny that. I'm simply saying, I feel you in this place.

How you choose to live your life, what you want to see, the experience of life around you, the abundance, the love, the joy, the health, it's all a reflection of your inner self. You will always see what you are looking for.

You have a really powerful mind. So you can look for amazing, self-sustaining communities that have permaculture gardens and all the rest and you can do it on either a shoestring budget or abundantly, feeling luxurious.

Neither is right or wrong. The choice is really yours.

But truly realize this… the choice is really yours. The more time you spend repelling money and wealth by thinking that you are a better person for doing it with less money, the more time you spend doing life with less money.

There really is no right or wrong. It's whatever story you have in your head telling you that it's so. But let's be real… it could just as easily tell you another truth. So I invite you to consider the one that is bringing you to all that you desire personally and in what you desire to give back. And know that you absolutely can do it from a space of abundance and where your cup is overflowing.

I know it may seem more complicated than this, but really you can have it all. It's just a matter of asking for it and walking towards it. No being on this planet is better than another – no matter their skin, religion, financial situation, sex, etc. It's simply conditioning.

And now that you realize that you have been programmed to believe the things you think, you can start to choose another reality, IF that's what you desire.

I mean… if you are in this spiritual community and want to stay broke, be my guest. Truly, no judgment.

If you want to serve and do your mission and ALSO be abundantly looked after, then by all means choose that.

There is no right or wrong, simply a choice.

So please watch yourself in the 'Mother Theresa – Martyrdom' complex, in which you think you have to be a martyr and give everything of yourself to be deemed worthy enough of having your dreams.

In doing that, you simply give your power away.

2. Family Legacy

This is the legacy you pass down to your children and the legacy of those who have walked before you.

Did you know that our DNA gets passed down SEVEN generations? That's quite the legacy you get to leave within your ancestral line. So what blueprint do you want to create?

I, for one, have been on my own personal journey to shift patterns and behaviors that have been passed on to me that are not serving me or my kids. I can see how I have passed things down that are unhelpful life skills, amongst some other amazing life skills.

THE NEW WEALTH

The cool thing is, nothing is permanent, so now we are all working to undo some of these behaviors and create a far more loving home in alignment with the principles of 'The New Wealth'.

People ask me about shifting ancestral patterns and I will share my thoughts on that here.

We are told that illness is passed down generation to generation through our DNA, which is seemingly true.

And here is my reality...

Our bodies are a tool to show us our energetic imbalances. My body is a guide for me to know where I am not in alignment with something because it starts talking to me and I listen.

Our body stores our emotions and our trauma. These are all part of our DNA that gets passed down from generation to generation.

The other thing to think about is that our 'mindset' and beliefs get passed down generationally.

And I believe that we create illness or dis-ease in our bodies because of the way we think, the way we speak to ourselves, the beliefs that we have, and whether they support us to be healthy, wealthy and moving through life with love or not.

So, as we choose to shift our consciousness, we choose to shift our mindset and our energy, and we let go of the bonds that tie us to a life of lack and limitation and struggle, we shift our DNA.

We shift the legacy that we leave for our family. We shift life for generations and generations to come.

It really is that important, the work that is happening on this planet right now. We get to choose a different way of being. We get to be a part of a major consciousness shift that is happening on this planet.

You can join in and choose to break the ancestral patterns that you are passing down generation to generation, 7 generations deep, or not.

Realize though, that simply by being here, on this planet at this time, and how you choose to show up, is in itself leaving a legacy that goes on for generations.

Again, it's important how you choose to show up in this iteration of life. It matters.

3. Financial Legacy

The more money you have, the more money you can give.

This is why it's important to learn to hold and grow your money, because the more you acquire it works for itself, and the compounding interest with more and more money is abundant and enjoyable to live on, and also allows you to continue to grow and grow your wealth so that you can give and give more.

This is not to say that you shouldn't give financially as you grow your wealth, by all means do. Sometimes, when I'm in my most dire moments financially, I will find a way to give financially that day or within days as it often gets me out of funks.

Give to receive.

THE NEW WEALTH

The question… can I leave a legacy if I don't have a lot of money? See the sections above. YES. You leave a massive legacy without spending a penny.

That said… if you want to be able to give to causes that you are passionate about, the more money you have, the more you can help them.

The amount of times that I have wanted to shake some of you, some absolutely brilliant minds with an absolutely amazing message to share with the world, and wake you up to how much you limit yourself in your ability to leave a financial legacy, is countless.

The more money you have, the more you can give, and the more you can give, the greater the impact you can make on the things that are important to you. And yet, you don't stand in your value and claim your Infinite Wealth so that you can make the contribution you deeply desire to make on this planet.

You push it away. You tell it that it's bad. You treat it like shit and so it stays away from you.

But imagine if you fell in love with your legacy and whatever means is necessary to leave the highest vibrational, energetic blueprint that you can. How would you show up for your purpose work on the planet then?

And also consider this…

If money is simply currency, and the currency of the planet, the literal vibration of the planet is LOVE, imagine how – when we spend our currency, our money – we are spreading love around the planet.

Imagine what would happen on the planet then. That makes my heart sing. What about you?

4. Global Legacy

This is the impact you have outside of you. The impact you have globally.

For some of you, that impact may remain in your local neighborhood and that is perfect.

For others, like me, you are here to reach the globe and create a global impact, and that is perfect.

For some of you, it will be somewhere in between.

Either way is perfect for you.

In global legacy, consider; what do you stand for?

What are you passionate about?

What cause would you want to stand up and speak about and serve?

Even if it's just within your family, start doing that. Then maybe it will be your neighbor. Then maybe it will be at a dinner party with 8 people and the next thing you know… the ripple goes on.

And how big you want that ripple to go on for is up to you. It's up to you to pick up that mic and that speaker and start preaching, if you feel called. By the way… just because it scares you to share about what's in your heart, doesn't mean it's not for you. ;-)

THE NEW WEALTH

It is scary to put your thoughts out into the public to see, to judge, to scrutinize. It does take courage. I say this because if it calls you, but you let the fear stop you, then you are limiting your impact on this world.

It's up to you to share ways to create a positive impact on the planet with others, if you choose. This is how you leave a Global Legacy.

As you grow your wealth, you may not choose to have a loud voice in leaving a legacy. That's ok.

You can leave a global legacy with where you invest your money and put your energy, too.

Use your voice with your money.

Buy products that are good for the earth. Invest in companies that are forward-thinking and are conscious of sustainability on Earth. Give your time and energy to causes that matter to you.

And here's an awareness I have recently owned… Your legacy can also be your business.

Over the last couple years, I have been grappling with myself around my lack of philanthropic endeavors and giving my time and energy to causes that are important to me, even though I'm deeply called to do some more philanthropic work.

I haven't found something that has felt like home yet and a place I deeply want to sink my energy into, and I have felt 'guilty' for not doing enough.

I have felt like I am not standing in my message around impact enough.

I have felt like I am letting my family down by not giving 'enough'.

And what I have chosen to believe instead is that my impact will be the greatest through my work right now.

This book, this movement, The New Wealth is my legacy. And right now, it's my dedication, my contribution to the planet and I give a lot of time and energy to this cause right now.

I know I have some more big philanthropic work in my future. I have already been guided to an inkling of what is to come, which is no small feat. But for now, my energy goes into this piece of my legacy.

I say this to give you permission to be the same.

Wherever you are right now on your journey of creating the impact you desire on this planet is absolutely perfect.

There is no tipping point. There is no end game here. It's a constant check-in to see, 'Am I living in alignment with the legacy I choose to leave?'

If the answer is yes… Perfect.

If the answer is 'No', then check in and re-align with your vision and take the next aligned action.

You are the most perfectly amazing being you can be right now on this planet.

And you always get to choose the impact that you create. What are you choosing?

LEGACY IS WHATEVER YOU WANT IT TO BE

So when I say, legacy can be whatever it is that is YOUR mission here, your Divine Call, then that is perfect.

Do not pressure yourself to be a thought leader with millions of followers, if that is not for you.

Do not pressure yourself to be anything that is not in alignment with you.

Do realize that whatever you do, you are leaving an energetic blueprint on this thread in time and that is your legacy.

Will you leave love or fear in your 'will'?

Take a moment to consider what is the energetic signature that you are leaving in the threads of time you are currently experiencing.

Are those the ripples you want to send into time and space? If so, then keep going. If not, then consider the blueprint you are choosing to leave and take the aligned actions towards that blueprint.

The problem that many of you face in leaving the legacy that, in your heart you want to leave, is that you don't believe you can. You don't think your 'little self' is worthy of anything legacy-like, and so you let the 'little you' win and you don't dream big enough.

On this bridge into The New Wealth, when you realize there truly is Infinite Abundance and you decide that you are worthy of every single one of your desires coming true – simply because you are here on this planet at this time... you will begin to tap into this Infinite Abundance.

Stop letting all those limiting beliefs around money or wealth speak to you anymore. Create new ones. Make them empowering and watch what happens.

You Make The Rules Up. Make Up Amazing Rules That Serve You.

Stop listening to the voice of the 'little you'. Your ego is keeping you small. It doesn't want change and doesn't like the unknown, and in order to leap you are going to have to step into the unknown, so stop listening to that small voice. Choose the big vision instead.

Break free from the box and dream big in what you desire in your life and in the impact you can have. Whatever you are thinking right now, times it by 10 and then go for it.

The only limitation you place on yourself is your own small mind. Shoot for the stars and keep shooting... never give up.

And know that as you clear the heavy energy that is clogging your field, stopping you from expanding yourself, you will get faster and faster at saying yes to your soul and allowing for the Divine co-creation that brings your dreams into reality.

You will begin to vibrate at the energy of LOVE, and that is what you will see, and that is the currency you become attuned to. LOVE.

And the more and more of us that embody this and choose this over and over again, the more we shift the vibration of the planet to LOVE. We change the entire way we show up on this planet and have a world based on LOVE.

THE NEW WEALTH

IT IS SO POSSIBLE. As a matter of fact, it is INEVITABLE. That is The New Wealth.

The New Wealth is a currency of LOVE.

Take a moment to imagine that world. It can be yours as easily as a world of fighting and anger and shame is. It's a choice.

The more of us that consistently choose LOVE, choose The New Wealth, we shift our whole planetary reality into the 5D, into New Wealth.

It will be done.

And those who are not open to adapting to this frequency of LOVE will be left behind. They will opt out, on purpose.

Over these next years, I predict that we will have more planetary catastrophes as Gaia brings The New Wealth down.

I predict this Coronavirus, the riots, the fires in Australia… all these horrific, catastrophic experiences that bring a horrendous death count to the planet are for a reason.

We are in a time of survival of the fittest. Those who can vibrationally shift their field to be in that of Love, Peace, Joy, Bliss and Abundance will stay on this Earthly plane. Those who can't will end up leaving their human body over the next years.

Please know that this has nothing to do with whether or not they are a good person. It's a contract they made to leave this planet and allow for the ascension.

Some have made a contract to move into the other realms to help us from those realms to bring in The New Wealth.

Either way… I predict we are going to see more and more catastrophic experiences as the people who are not able to make the ascension into The New Wealth leave the planet.

I'm not saying this to be horrible. There are people in my life that I don't want to see go, and yet, we all will go whenever our time is up. That is the biggest truth I know along with the sun rises in the morning, eventually we all die. So, I don't fear death. My greatest wish is that neither will you. It gives you the freedom to truly live.

MY LEGACY

My whole life I have been a peacemaker. Everywhere I go, I just want peace.

My greatest wish, my biggest dream is that in my lifetime, PEACE and LOVE reign over this planet, individually and collectively.

My deepest desire for humanity is that we all choose LOVE and PEACE.

If we all took full and complete responsibility for our own actions, we would live in a world of PEACE and LOVE in the most empowered way. I have believed that for about 14 years. And now I see it happening before my eyes. It can happen in this lifetime.

This Is 'The New Wealth'.

This is the Legacy that I am leaving on this Earth, in this moment of time. This movement towards a New Wealth. This movement towards LOVE.

I am walking through the fire to burn down everything that no longer serves me to bring The New Wealth to this planet and to help us all make the transition to the currency of LOVE.

So, if you can just try this on, even if you are not ready to believe that this world exists, just try it on for a few minutes. Then, see if you can wear it a bit longer each day until it's in your cells, too, and you realize that we live in a world of Infinite Abundance and you get to make the rules.

Let abundance and love be a part of your legacy too. Choose it. Right here and now. Choose Love. Choose Abundance. Choose Pleasure. Choose Joy.

You get to have it all.

You get to feel good!

And as you just slowly try this on… and look through the lens of peace, joy, abundance, bliss, and joy, what do you see?

Allow yourself to dream, without limitations. Not later. Now. Close your eyes. Really. Do it. Ok… read what to do first and then close your eyes. Right away. Do the thing. ;-)

Ok… so close your eyes and see what is around you when you are embodying the life of Love, Joy, Bliss, Peace, and Abundance.

You may not see anything. Maybe you will sense it, feel it, hear it… however it shows up for you, become aware of your surroundings as you allow your life to be so amazing.

Feel the energy of that. Sense into that energetic blueprint. Is it one that feels good to be leaving behind or paying it forward, as the case may be?

What do you stand so strongly in belief around that you have the conviction to drive energy and money to improve that experience on the planet and bring it to the vibration of love?

Do that. Leave your mark. The one that calls to you.

Connect with your Divine Purpose and let it move you. Say yes to your soul.

THE NEW WEALTH

Every day, take one more step closer to this vision and let's walk to The New Wealth together.

It's here for you.

Are you ready to join the Re-Evolution?

Welcome to The New Wealth.

You are welcome here.

REVIEW

Four Types of Legacy

1. **Energetic**
   A. Your own energetic blueprint.
   B. Giving your time and energy.

2. **Family**
   Ancestral conditioning passed down from generation to generation.

3. **Financial**
   The more you make, the more you can give to the causes that are important to you.

4. **Global**
   A. SPEAK. Use your voice.
   B. Use your money to buy in ways that support your values and support causes that are important to you.

Legacy is whatever you want to make it. You get to choose. And by BEing you and living into your Divine Blueprint, you leave an energetic signature on this planet. Be mindful of the blueprint you are leaving. It matters.

Remember to do this activation:

Close your eyes and see what is around you when you are embodying the life of Love, Bliss, Peace, Abundance and Joy. You may not see anything. Maybe you will sense it, feel it, hear it… however it shows up for you, become aware of your surroundings as you allow your life to be so amazing.

THE NEW WEALTH

> Feel the energy of that. Sense into that energetic blueprint. Is it one that feels good to be leaving behind or paying it forward, as the case may be?
>
> What do you stand for so strongly that you have the conviction to drive energy and money to improve that experience on the planet, and bring it to the vibration of love?
>
> Do that. Leave your mark. The one that calls to you.
>
> Connect with your Divine Purpose and let it move you. Say yes to your soul.

ACTIVATION QUESTIONS:

Questions to ponder for yourself or to discuss at a book club.

1. What are your 2 top takeaways from this section that – if you were to embody and implement them into your life – would allow you to shift closer to your dreams?

2. What was activated within you? Where is there a new spark of light guiding you?

   What is that spark guiding you towards?

3. What do you value in life or what is important to you that you would like to be able to support even more?

   For example: The environment, child trafficking, domestic abuse, health advocacy, etc… What fires you up so much that you want to take action and make a difference to the lives of others?

4. Now that you are thinking about how important your energetic blueprint is on this planet, what is the legacy you want to leave behind? Who do you choose to be? Journal on this. Write as much as you can about the person you choose to be in all areas of your life.

5. Now, look at your life and consider, are you showing up that way right now? What changes can you make to shift the way you show up in this world?

6. What support do you need/desire in order to be the person who leaves the Divine legacy you are here to bring to this planet?

SECTION 7
THE CURRENCY IN THE NEW WEALTH

Whilst I have no 'guarantee' that this is right, in my nearly 2 decades of reading and studying energy, and constantly knowing things before they happen and building a solid relationship with my intuition, I am willing to put this prediction into a book.

And, again, I simply invite you to look deeper into the truths that are all around you on the planet at this time, if you are willing to look.

You have been trapped in a 3D matrix, as have I. Trapped into the fear, greed, corruption, manipulation, judgment, lack, fighting, etc.

It sucks. We are a humanity that is literally living in hellish circumstances when you consider what is possible. And we have been living in a bubble that has kept us trapped from seeing the truth. We have been purposefully led like sheep into lack, scarcity, debt, dependency, and financial slavery.

It is time to stand up and say NO MORE.

It is time to wake up to the games that are going on around us. Please know that what I have touched on in this book is really only the beginning of the truth behind our financial system on the planet right now.

And right now, we have a choice.

THE NEW WEALTH

We have a choice to remain plugged into the 3D matrix and all the stuff that you don't like about life.

Or we can choose to transcend it.

The etymology of transcendence is from Latin *transcendentem* (nominative *transcendens*) and means 'surmounting, rising above'. https://www.etymonline.com/word/transcendent

It means that you get to allow yourself to take on a whole new set of beliefs and ways of showing up in the world and rise above this chaos on the planet right now.

It means that you get to learn to shift your energetic vibration so that you can raise it to that of LOVE. What a gift, hey? To realize that is the path in front of you is to learn to live in the vibration of LOVE.

When I speak of Love, I ask you to consider what love is in the purest form, without condition. In our current 3D reality, many of us have experienced a very toxic, conditional love in this lifetime.

Love has equaled pain and trauma for most of us at some point or another. So, the work in front of us is to clear our physical, mental, emotional, spiritual, and energetic bodies of the stored trauma and energy that is keeping us looping in this toxic existence of love.

It will take inner work, which means time and energy and a financial investment in yourself for you to live in this pure space of love. It is a choice. Especially right now, as we ascend our consciousness, it's likely a daily choice.

As you begin your journey to choose this, it can be a moment-to-moment choice because it's easy to fall back into the negative collective consciousness and your past conditioning.

Remember with all of this ascension that is happening right now, personally and globally, there are no guarantees, but look at what you are striving for. How could it be bad?

We get to do our best to live and experience life in the vibration of Love, Abundance, Wealth, Joy, Bliss and Gratitude.

I wish that experience of life for everyone. It is available for all of us. First, we all must CHOOSE it.

Remember what I have said throughout the whole book… It starts with a DECISION, which is to cut apart from any other way.

We all get to DECIDE that this current reality of life is no longer working for us and then RISE above it.

It takes the ability to look at it all from a bird's eye view, take in all the information, and then come to your own conclusions.

Start by doing your own research around the current financial systems to get a deeper understanding of what our truth is right now.

Search for things like:

- Bail-out and Bail-in and see how the banking systems can freeze your money.
- Federal Reserve
- Central Banks
- International Monetary Fund

- Check out books by Nomi Prins. I have only gotten to Collusion by the time of writing this, but there are some other good ones too.
- Global Financial Elite
- Who owns the Central Banks?
- NESARA and GESARA are interesting concepts around eliminating debt. I don't know that they will come to fruition, but have a look into it.
- Wherever else the path takes you… And it will take you, I'm sure.

Go to duckduckgo, which is a search engine, to do your online research. It will allow you to get a more uncensored view of what is going on in the world right now.

I also recommend you do some research on Ascension principles. This may or may not be the first time you have come across this concept. I'm not alone when talking about these principles. There is so much amazing information on ascension.

You can begin to search for topics like:

- Ascension.
- 3D, 5D, 4D Bridge.
- Starseeds.
- Steven Greer talks about extraterrestrial beings.
- I invite you to open yourself up to the concept of developing a deep relationship with your intuition and also realize that you have 'psychic gifts'. We all have the ability to fine tune our sense of hearing, seeing, sensing, and feeling.

    Maybe you know you have these abilities. Maybe you never realized you could do this. Maybe you think being psychic is something outside of you and you leave it to the other people to do that.

    Maybe you have visited a psychic once to predict your future and thought, how did they do that?

Either way is perfect. Just start to know that we ALL have this ability, and the more you tap into these gifts, the easier it will be for you to be Divinely guided in your life and ascend into The New Wealth.

There is a bonus training to help you discover how to tap deeper into your intuition. To get it, head over to www.kerinorley.com/resources.

- Quantum Physics:
There is tons out there on this. I highly suggest you read 'Becoming Supernatural' by Joe Dispenza, and if you are not new to meditation, get some of his meditations and do them.

- Meditation:
If you aren't meditating, start. For 1 minute, for 5 minutes, for 10 minutes. Learn about this practice. It's more than just sitting and getting annoyed that your mind is still chattering.

Even doing the dishes can be a meditation, so can going for a bike ride, or sitting and listening to a guided meditation. There are so many variations and ways to do this.

Ultimately, you are just wanting to do your best to quiet the mind. Thoughts will come, thoughts will go. Learn to be an observer of your thoughts instead of attaching to them.

- Quantum Flow:
I have mentioned this throughout the book. It's an embodiment practice that clears your field on all levels to remove stored energy in the body and help free you from toxic, looping behaviors.

You can experience Quantum Flow here www.kerinorley.com/resources

Please make sure you go do this. It can transform your life.

THE NEW WEALTH

This will get you started. Allow yourself to follow where the path leads you. It's a fun rabbit hole to dive down and way more empowering than watching TV and staying tapped into the control and manipulation of media.

Come join me in my Telegram chat where I share current, relevant information in regard to these topics and raising your vibrations.

If you don't know what Telegram is, it's a messaging communication app that at the time of writing this is a secure place to connect, not be heard by government or other people listening into our conversations and we can talk freely without being censored.

You can join me here: https://t.me/wealthalchemist

In all ways right now, you are being asked to ask the bigger, deeper questions. Do this in the world of finance and money and see if you think it is rigged in your favour or someone else's favour.

Do this in all areas of life and really examine the current systems we have in place for 'health', education, and relating.

Are they actually empowering?

Or are they all designed to control us and make us like sheep that follow the rules? The rules keep us controllable, numb and unable to think for ourselves. This is exactly what the powers that be want from us, in this earthly plane and beyond.

Here we are again, we get to DECIDE.

Is this what we want?

Or do we choose the life of Bliss and Abundance, Joy and Wealth and Love? Keep remembering, it's always a choice!

I find it so strange that it seems scarier to choose the life of Love and Infinite Abundance than it is to stay trapped in the same slavery/fear consciousness paradigm. And yet, that is often the case for myself and the people I have spoken to about walking through the barriers to this life and likely for you too.

I mean, it makes sense when we have been programmed to believe that this mecca couldn't possibly exist. It is challenging for the human mind to comprehend that we could live in such a glorious experience of life.

I mean… imagine it…

A world where:

- PEACE prevails.
- We love and honour each Being on this planet.
- Everyone is abundantly looked after.
- We vibrate Love.
- We are healthful, vibrant, energetic beings.
- We positively contribute to society.
- We get to have fun and feel good.
- We are all Sovereign Beings.
- We have True Freedom.

In some ways, it's hard to imagine such a place because we are conditioned to believe that it cannot exist.

In this current reality, with these current systems and this consciousness, in which we are slaves within the boxes that have been created for us, it cannot exist.

It takes elevating your thoughts, your energy, your physical body, your spiritual body and your emotional state, to shift out of this limited matrix and move into The New Wealth.

THE NEW WEALTH

Let it be known... this decision is here for you. This way of life awaits you, it is the way forward, but it comes at a cost.

You will have to work through your own limitations and patterns that are keeping you Addicted to Suffering. It's these addictions that will keep you trapped in the 3D matrix. But freeing yourself of them will give you the ability to rise above.

This bridge is a critical piece of the ascension. It will take Earthly time and it will ask you to look deep into your shadows to alchemize the limitations lurking in them.

If you want to set yourself free... please get guidance in walking this path.

I have ways to help you. You can find more information about my programs and mentoring at the back of the book. And there are other Great Awakeners on the planet that will also help you.

This awakening is not to be done alone.

This awakening takes a community to support you, and then we all must choose it together.

Allow yourself to receive guidance from multiple people and PLEASE be DISCERNING about who you work with. It's hard to know who to follow, who to trust, who to listen to right now. I get that.

Everything is in so much unrest and it's hard to know where to turn.

I say turn everywhere. You will learn through listening to someone, and implementing and seeing what happens for you each step of the way. Every bit counts. Every lesson learned is perfect.

I say open your eyes and heart to see all the pieces to the puzzle. What would happen if you took your dark glasses off so that you can truly see what's going on from a far broader perspective?

Maybe nothing will happen and you will think this a load of BS, which is totally your choice. I'm guessing you didn't get this far in the book if that's your thought process though.

So you must be either a full 'yes' to making this leap, nodding your head all the way or maybe you are just slightly open to the fact that this is possible. Either way, just start taking the steps.

Be willing to fall flat on your face, 'cause you likely will, many times.

Every step of the way, just listen in for what feels aligned to you in each moment.

BONUS: Come and have a listen to my training on Following Your Intuition here www.kerinorley.com/resources.

Learning to hear and ACT on your intuition is a crucial piece to your ascension. Please do yourself a favor and take the time to listen to this and to implement acting on your intuitive knowing into your life. It's the path to your soul alignment.

WHAT WILL BE THE CURRENCY IN THE NEW WEALTH?

CRYPTOCURRENCY

Well, at the time of writing this book… there is no doubt in my mind that Digital Currency will be some aspect of the future.

We have countries adopting it into their financial system. We have banking systems utilising it.

It makes sense.

The reality is that our currency is all digital now too, even in the fiat currency. There are not as many pieces of paper or coins in the marketplace as there are numbers in a computer system. We transfer money digitally now all the time.

The difference between our current fiat system and cryptocurrency is:

Crypto is secure, so that it cannot be tracked or tampered with by the government. Let me be clear on this aspect. There is decentralized crypto that cannot be tampered with by the government.

At the time of writing this there are countries looking to adopt this too. So I'm assuming that the cryptocurrency that some governments roll out will be traceable and controllable by the government, and probably still the financial elite at some level. So, be mindful of this and question everything as we move forward.

Crypto is for the people. It is here to help us create our own sovereignty. Of course, remembering the note above… as governments bring this in, do your research and take the time to learn about this so that you buy into the system that is designed for you to have your own financial sovereignty.

Also realizing that people with not so good intentions can get into this space and create scams and fraudulent experiences. I purposefully recommend people to work with at the back of the book so that you can trust them and know you are working with people of integrity, if you want to dive deeper into this work.

Yes. I kinda feel like the Digital currency space is a bit like the Wild West. It's a new system and some coins are succeeding and some are not. But you cannot turn a blind eye to this anymore.

Cryptocurrency is being adopted into governments and banking systems. It's not a matter of 'will this happen' anymore, it is happening before our eyes. You can turn a blind eye to it and say it's the wild west and too risky to get involved in, or you can take time to learn about it and become friends with it, 'cause it's not going anywhere.

It's coming towards us.

NOW is the time to learn about it and start putting some money in it, if you want to be an early adopter and have the potential for much bigger gains then you will if you invest in a few years time. And, please get educated to do this as there is a learning curve to play in this space and make money.

I don't know that it is the be all and end all of currency in 'The New Wealth' but it certainly is here right now.

I'm gonna say this time and time again... I'm not a financial advisor. I'm not an expert in crypto or alternative finance. I am learning, too. I am just sharing with you some of the amazing things I am finding along the way as we embark into a new system of currency.

Speaking of a new system of currency... the next section that I am going to share with you is blowing my mind. Read on to find out about Decentralized Finance.

DECENTRALIZED FINANCE

This excites me in every cell of my body. As I wrote this book and envisioned this future, I knew we had crypto as a means for exchange, but there is a lot of instability in that and also a lack of liquidity in that space. Liquidity meaning, you can access your cash and spend it now.

With a bunch of the coins, you are asked to put money in and leave it there for growth of the coin. Also, at this point you have to be in certain coins to be able to use it for daily transactions.

It has its limitations right now, so I wrote this book wondering what would show up to be able to 're-create' a banking system without using the current banks, trusting that it would happen.

And before even going to edit on this book, an amazing string of events brought me to connecting with Rossco Paddison about Decentralized Finance or DeFi. If you haven't checked out our first interview on the current financial system yet, please do.

We also have an interview to listen to about Decentralized Finance. You can check both of them out here: www.kerinorley.com/resources

As I bring this book to the world, I am diving deep into this because I believe it is an amazing way of the future for those of you who want a way to be your own financially sovereign being.

What does financial sovereignty actually mean? That you are not reliant on anyone else to hold and manage your money. You are totally responsible for it. This is amazing!

THE NEW WEALTH

In Decentralized Finance, at the time of printing this, you have the ability to make approximately 7.5%-8.5% compounding interest AND it's liquid. Meaning, you can transact with it right now.

So, you can move your fiat currency (dollars) into the DeFi space and get a card to access your accounts and spend it in shops, like you would a normal bank card. It's not trapped anywhere, so you can get access to it whenever you need it.

Eventually, it is said we will be able to get loans for a mortgage or other big investments through this space too.

The difference being, the Global Financial Elite don't control this and don't make the money from holding our money, we do.

Seems too good to be true? It's not.

If you listen to the interview I did with Rossco about the current financial system, we talk about how banks make their money. Remember, they charge high interest rates for credit and lower but still interest for mortgages and other loans.

We get maybe .5-1% in our savings accounts from banks. Where does the rest go if they are making anywhere from 4%-22% interest in what we pay them in interest? To the banks.

In DeFi, that interest goes to us. The people. We become sovereign.

Please make sure to check out our interview to drop deeper into how this works. Like I said… it's a new world to me, but Rossco has been living and breathing this for the past 3 years and will blow your mind at what is possible.

Again… here is the link for the interviews: www.kerinorley.com/resources

If you want to start learning more about this and be able to play in this space yourself, you can go here to learn more.

Rossco has created an amazing and simple program to teach you everything you need to know to play in DeFi. You can get yourself set-up and going within a short amount of time. Details for this are also at www.kerinorley.com/resources

DeFi is quickly becoming something I love and I'm fascinated with. I see this as being how we can move forward in a sovereign way around our own finances.

Even if this seems risky or too good to be true to you, I invite you to simply check it out. Be willing to open yourself to a new possibility.

When electricity was created and the car was invented, etc they were new too and were risky and too good to be true. Now they are a completely normal part of our lives that none of us can imagine living with out. Please remember that as you dive into the world of DeFi.

OTHER POSSIBILITIES FOR FINANCIAL MOVEMENTS

There are a few other interesting movements around that I have not had enough time to check out, yet, to really give you more information right now.

NESARA and GESARA, which I mentioned earlier, these are movements to eliminate debt around the globe.

There is also Universal Basic Income, which states that we all get enough money to pay for our 'basic needs'.

I don't know that this will take off either and it doesn't really create sovereignty, but I do want you to see that there are people in the world that are bringing ideas to the planet that will mean a different experience to money than we currently have.

I'm sure there are more if you go digging, but all of what I have shared here will get you started in a new currency for the world and give you plenty to learn about for now.

WE ARE MOVING FORWARD

No matter how you look at it, things are moving forward. There are glimmers of hope for the future of our financial ecosystem that will support us in abundance, and the currency of love, and becoming Sovereign Beings.

If you take the time to learn about these alternatives in currency, you have the potential to change your entire financial reality with smart decisions and long-term strategy.

Again, I am NOT a financial advisor, so of course speak to your advisor and do your own research.

Also… if you are looking to learn about Crypto, there are many people teaching it out there. I would highly recommend talking to someone who knows about digital currency but also understands the current financial system too. Preferably one that actually understands the energetics of the world as well.

Getting a mentor to guide you through this will save you thousands of hours and probably thousands of dollars too. It really is a bit like the Wild West out there, so go into it with people who are already creating financial success from it.

I have included referrals for people to learn from in the back of the book if you want to know more about the crypto space. This is definitely not something you want to do alone.

I believe in my heart that if we ALL choose this way of life that Peace on Earth can happen in my lifetime. I mean, why not?

THE NEW WEALTH

I believe that we all have this life as our Divine Birthright and we all get to choose it. I know it's kinda hard to wrap your logical mind around this because history tells us that it's not possible.

But hey… we get to write our own stories, so pick the story you want.

I will say it again, I cannot guarantee anything. I have just spent many years learning to read and shift energy, mindset, and human behavior, and I'm being very strongly shown this. The more and more I dig into the concepts presented in this book, the less I can hide from them.

The more I embrace this as truth, the better and better my life gets.

Who knows what will happen globally as you step into this way of life? But it will be a road that leads YOU to Love, Abundance, Joy, Bliss, and Gratitude, so that's a good thing, hey?

I invite you to walk this path alongside me.

Let's pave the road to 'The New Wealth'.

REVIEW

There is a new currency coming for us to live in 'The New Wealth'. We get to have financial sovereignty and take our power back.

The first thing to remember is that ultimately, our greatest currency is our personal energy. It's important to the world to bring your own vibration to that of love, abundance, bliss, joy and peace.

As far as the financial system goes, two of the ways currently available for us to begin to use an alternative to the traditional banking system are Cryptocurrency and Decentralized Finance, which is ultimately a part of the cryptocurrency space.

Do your research. Start learning. Invest what feels good for you.

Remember what we talked about in the section about holding wealth. This is an investment. Begin to invest in your future and the future of humanity.

And remember what we talked about in the legacy section and know that you get to put your money where you value and with that, leave a legacy.

You get to be a part of changing the financial reality for yourself and humanity.

ACTIVATION QUESTIONS:

Questions to ponder for yourself or to discuss at a book club.

1. What are your 2 top takeaways from this section that – if you were to embody and implement them into your life – would allow you to shift closer to your dreams?

2. What was activated within you? Where is there a new spark of light guiding you?

3. What is that spark guiding you towards?

4. What does the experience of unconditional love look and feel like for you? What is keeping you from experiencing that right now?

5. What steps will you take to clear anything from your life that is NOT pure, unconditional love? This will take untangling and clearing your field from ancestral and current life trauma. This is your work. It is all of our work on the planet right now.

6. What are your thoughts on the new currency coming to the world? Are you already involved in the cryptocurrency space? What about DeFi? Where do you lean towards to discover more first? Is this all new to you? What have you taken away so far? What's your next aligned action in moving towards the new currency?

SECTION 8

BONUS: WHAT DO YOU DO WHEN YOUR PARTNER ISN'T WANTING ANYTHING TO DO WITH THIS WORK?

If you are with a partner in life, bring these conversations to them. Invite them into this conversation. It's not always easy having financial conversations between partners, but it's MANDATORY for a relationship. AND… the power that you have in bringing the currency in together is even more magnetic.

I get asked this question A LOT.

How do I become magnetic when my partner doesn't believe in any of this?

Earlier in the book, I talked about Self-Mastery for Self-Sovereignty. The whole point is that you are the master of your own energy field and no one that isn't welcomed in gets to influence that.

So, if you want to manifest a bigger dream than your partner, if you dive deeper into this work than that person, if you are waking up and they are still sound asleep… just keep doing you.

Always come back to and just keep doing you. Your partner will either choose to walk the path with you or they won't.

Then ultimately, it's your decision as to whether that serves you or not. There is no right or wrong in this.

Big, Huge Hint In Working Through Relationship Stuff...

LOOK AT YOUR MIRROR REFLECTION

****. This may be a hard pill to swallow but when you truly embody this into your life, it will completely transform.

Before you do lose faith and leave them because you are so over it, look at yourself.

Where are you doing the same exact thing that you are annoyed that they are doing?

We are all mirror reflections of each other. The ones closest to us are often the most painful reflection when we are beating ourselves up, because you just keep beating up on each other.

So, your work is to see your magnificent self in them. Start looking for the amazing. Look for the magic.

Start creating it in your life and let it wash around those that you love. Do it unconditionally.

Do it with love for yourself and the knowing that the more you shine, the more those around you will either rise up to meet you, or fall away. Either way… it's perfect.

Let go of the attachment that you have to an outcome. Do you. Consistently and unconditionally do you.

I said to my husband a couple of years ago, as I sat in that exact same place and demanded more in our relationship, 'We will either walk out of this divorced, or we will walk out of this in such beautiful and full alignment with ourselves and our relationship, and we will be teaching this work.'

Either way is perfect, by the way. For us, it has been a really hard road. I'm not going to pretend this work is easy.

Manifesting a new relationship as you evolve and calling in someone new to match your vibration is in some ways more simple, not easier, than re-defining a 15-year relationship because the people we are with hold us to the way they have seen us for years, so even as we evolve, the patterns we have played will want to keep us trapped.

There has been more than one time that I have wanted more out of our marriage. We became so horrible to each other. It was not one of us. We played out all the most horrible patterns from our parents' relationship.

We had to decide to re-define the relationship and create one of LOVE.

I finally looked at him one day over this time in Covid lockdown after years and years of asking for him to be the best version of himself and for our bickering to end and said,

'I'm tired of this story. I'm tired of this loop. I would rather be thinking and feeling love. I would rather be talking about our dreams coming to life. I would rather talk about how amazing the intimacy we are having is and how we can make it even better. I would rather play games and giggle with you.'

And finally he got that my desire to see him shift his energy wasn't because he isn't amazing.

It's because I love him so deeply and think that he is one of the most amazing beings on this planet. Truly I do. I am so supported in so many ways by my husband and I am blessed to have him in my life.

We just spent a lot of years treating each other horribly.

We finally chose differently and everything in our lives is turning around in the most magical way. And together we both keep saying yes.

We are still working through stuff, but we are working through it.

So, I'm saying this to you to say… never give up on that experience, whether you are in a relationship or calling one in.

You get to have a Divine Union with a being that you share love with and that you get to co-create with.

In the meantime, work on your own Divine Union. Work on the marriage of your own inner masculine and inner feminine. I do this work with my clients. It's pivotal work to your self-mastery.

In case you don't know… it doesn't matter whether we are a man or a woman, we have a masculine and feminine energy within each of us and we get to cultivate a relationship with both our inner masculine and feminine. And as we do, and we grow those parts of ourselves up, and we learn to honour and respect those parts of ourselves, the more we see that reflection in the outside world.

For many women and men, this shows up in this day and age as living from your masculine and forgetting the power of your feminine and being totally disconnected from your magic.

And... your inner masculine is likely acting like a teenage boy wanting to drive and hunt and go stick his penis into everything. And he's spraying that energy all around the world. That energy gets to grow up and mature within you as much as it does the man or woman that you are seeking.

The same goes for your Divine Feminine. She's likely acting like a little child and whining and tantruming when she doesn't get her way.

She could be in her teens/twenties and prostituting herself, with or without sex, but completely allowing herself to receive whatever comes her way without any boundaries. It feels like you are constantly being fucked and not in the good way.

It will show up in your intimate life and also in your life... getting screwed over by other people and you think it's the other person being the horrid one. But really, take a cold, hard look at yourself and see how you are allowing it.

Everything in your life is there because it is a mirror reflection of you. This can be a really hard pill to swallow when you truly embody this.

If you do not like what you are seeing, change the channel. Look for new things to watch and allow yourself to see them.

THE NEW WEALTH

Your journey with your relationship around your own Divine Union will either make or break your relationship, and either way is perfect.

On that journey, you are allowing yourself to magnetize your dreams to you. Your partner doesn't get to influence that, unless you want them to. This is where your boundaries need to be impeccable.

This is a journey and we are all still human and let things slide. Just pay attention that you don't play the pushover. I invite you to Stand in your fullest power and see what blossoms from there. This journey into our own Divine Union is one that can be done together. It's crucial for the ability to live in The New Wealth.

Whether you have a partner or not, this Divine Union is for you. Are you ready to fall in love with you?

You've got this! Keep looking at that reflection, keep looking within, and keep moving forward.

SECTION 9
WELCOME TO 'THE NEW WEALTH'

This book is a Divine transmission. This is an awakening into your soul. Since you have read this far, something has awoken within you. And your life has been altered in the most amazing way. And when you take any of these things that you learned and implement it, you have the opportunity for magic to happen.

If this is your first time receiving an activation like this, then realize it can take some time for your field to acclimatize. Let it move you. Let it sink into your cells. Let yourself embody what the pages have activated within you.

And know that this is only the first step.

Read this again. Come back to it often. Each time you will receive something new. There are many layers to this book.

Just a few short months ago, I had the call to write a book. Truthfully, when I said yes to my guidance and the opportunities that presented themselves to me, I had no idea this is what would be released from my fingers, that this is what would channel through me.

I just knew that the world was in chaos and more and more people were leaning into fear and scarcity than calling in abundance and love, and I knew that it was my job to be a pillar for abundance and wealth, and to guide people through this chaos into an even more beautiful experience of life.

THE NEW WEALTH

We have been trapped in our homes, asked to face our own stuff, been thrown into new conversations, juggling kids and work, been separated and isolated.

We have had freedoms taken away from us. We have been censored on social media. The list goes on.

We are in unprecedented times. The veil is getting thinner. We are seeing more than we have ever seen before.

We have more power than ever before to stand for ourselves and use our voices, our money, our energy to raise the consciousness of the planet.

We can see everything going on around us and fall victim to it, hoping that somehow it gets better.

You can give your power away to all the stuff going on around you.

Or, you can rise up.

You can see it all for what it is and know that you have a choice to not buy into it.

It doesn't matter where you look at this point in time. There are multiple sides to every story. There is 'proof' for every angle.

You can convince yourself that all of what I have said so far is a load of crap and a big lie.

You can think that the banking system is amazing and serves you.

You can think that the government is here for your best interest.

You can think that pharmaceutical companies are here to help you 'heal' and feel better.

You can think the education system is a great place to send your kids to get the education they need to move ahead in their life.

You can buy into the corruption, greed and manipulation.

All of this is here for you, and there is proof that all of that is true, if you go looking for it. That also doesn't make it a life of Sovereignty, Bliss, Abundance and Love.

You can also read this and resonate with what I am saying. Maybe, even if it triggers you and you don't know if you can believe this or not, you can open your mind to the possibility.

You can believe that there is a financial system that will allow you to become fully sovereign with your finances.

You can think that the government may have some good people in there, but at the core, it is full of lies, deception and greed, and you may desire a way to live that is truly of the people and for the people.

You can think that natural, holistic health is the way to go.

You can believe that vibrational frequency devices are the way of our future and can help the planet, as a whole, to be a healthier, higher vibrational species.

You can look at the general education system and realize it breeds robots and teaches people not to think for themselves, but to get a job and become a slave to the system.

THE NEW WEALTH

You can buy into The New Wealth and a new way of BEing on this planet.

Whatever it is you look for, you will find evidence to support it.

For you to walk in alignment moving forward and get out of the conditioning of slavery and suffering that we are currently all made to believe is the way life has to be, you get to tap into your heart and soul and ask yourself the tough questions. You get to listen to the call and where it is pulling you.

Either way, you are right.

For me, the whole intention of getting this book to you and introducing you to the movement of The New Wealth is with the hopes that you open up to a new possibility.

However you are feeling about this concept right now, all in or still a bit on the fence, I just invite you to see the world through New Eyes. I invite you to look beyond the noise that is distracting you from the truth. I invite you to follow your heart.

If you have gotten this far, I commend you. If you have gotten this far, I know that this has stirred something in your soul and so I ask, what are you going to do now?

Are you going to close this book and forget what you read in the pages?

Are you going to close this book and go on with your life in the same way you have done before?

Are you going to close this book and fall back asleep?

Or, are you going to close this book, knowing this is an opening, not a closing at all?

What are you willing to open yourself to right now?

What are you willing to do in order to remove the limitations, energy and beliefs that keep you trapped in the 3D experience of Suffering?

Moving into the 5D – moving into 'The New Wealth', into a space of love, bliss, joy, abundance, peace, and wealth – is a choice.

Remember this choice moment to moment.

Take a moment now to breathe it in.

Breathe in what life looks like when you are Free. Breathe in what life looks like when you become fully Sovereign.

See what you see, hear what you hear, feel all the amazing feelings of that life and choose it over and over again. Choose it NOW.

This is the biggest work you can do right now. And not only choose it for yourself… join me and the other activators in spreading this message.

Tell people about this book. If you haven't already, start a book club with your friends and read this book together. Keep each other accountable to this new way of being.

Begin to live this way and together we rise.

THE NEW WEALTH

It takes each and every individual to say yes to this to completely shift the consciousness of the planet.

Together we rise.

And together, we can do this.

I fully and firmly believe that.

It is going to challenge you. It is going to ask you to step outside of your comfort zone, but hey, I'm willing to trade in some discomfort now to bring through this consciousness and live in a completely different reality in the future, for myself and for my kids and for future generations to come.

And heck, isn't it uncomfortable no matter how you look at it, right now?

Together we rise.

Are you with me?

If you have said yes to being with me, please join me in moving forward in this movement.

It is an honour to lead you to 'The New Wealth'.

MOVING FORWARD IN 'THE NEW WEALTH'

If you are called to take the next step with me, then listen to that call and join me in any of these ways:

Wealth Alchemy Programs

WEALTH CODES

Have you had enough of your BS money stories keeping you stuck and stagnant and not moving forward in your ability to create wealth or make the money you desire?

Are you ready to take your financial experience of life to the next level?

This is the space for you.

There are codes for everything. Just like a computer programmer puts some numbers into a system and out comes an image or words or numbers, we can code ourselves to Wealth.

We can program our system to be in the energy of Wealth.

- Drop into the Energetics of Creating a container that allows you to RECEIVE everything you desire.
- We dive into your personal blueprint for creating wealth.

THE NEW WEALTH

- Begin to reset your Nervous System to allow your body to have the space to bring through your manifestations now.

- Bring in New Wealth Codes and Re-Wire your DNA to tap into Infinite Abundance.

- Clear Looping patterns around money.

- Discover your Human Design and how that effects your wealth creation

- Feng Shui for Abundance

- How to get started in DeCentralised Finance

- Look at what it takes to bust through that invisible glass ceiling you have placed on yourself.

- And more...

This is an incredibly powerful experiential container that will have you clearing that which no longer serves you, so that you can create your next-level dreams.

Results:
- One client massively stretched her goal, which was to hit $100,000, and she did it.

- One wanted to start a coaching practice and start generating income from that. He wrote a book, brought on his first 4 new clients, and increased his commitment to savings/wealth growth substantially.

- One client hit her target for the 6 weeks in the first week!

For more information about this program head over to www.kerinorley.com/wealthcodes

WEALTH AMPLIFIER

This is for you if:

- you have or will be inheriting money,
- if you have been through a divorce and received your settlement and you have never been the one to deal with finances, or
- if you are an entrepreneur who is increasing your income and finally hitting 5-figure+ launches/months, and the money is going out as fast as it's coming in.
- Or, if you are a human on the planet that has struggled to hold onto your money. It goes out as fast as it comes in.

In this program we dive deeper into the energetics of being able to hold your money. And I will start to talk to you about legacy work and what you get to think about now that you have extra money.

Celebrate. This is a great place to be.

I'm going to show you how to fall in love with this journey and not feel overwhelmed by it.

I have not found anything like this on the market. I know. I looked long and hard and never found it. Everything I wish I knew about receiving a ton of money and how to energetically hold and grow it is in here.

Subjects we will cover are:

- Where are you prostituting yourself? Trust me... if you haven't looked at this piece it will likely change the game for you.
- Money spending and Managing your money.

- Philanthropy.

- Diving deep into a whole new level of TRUST, FAITH, and SURRENDER.

- Attaching and detaching to money and the outcome.

- Financial security.

- And more…

I will NOT just be talking about these topics. I will be taking you through energetic and emotional clearing on the quantum level that will completely allow you to let go of that which is no longer serving you.

Ultimately, in this program I am helping you create your own Financial Sovereignty.

You can get more information here: www.kerinorley.com/wealthamplifier

ONE-ON-ONE WORK

I take a limited amount of one-on-one clients to work with to re-pattern their experience of money and wealth and move into a new level of playing life.

It's a beautiful and transformational experience to work with me over time to completely transform your reality.

If you are feeling called to this, please feel free to reach out to me and see if we are an aligned fit to work together by heading here: www.kerinorley.com/workwithme

OTHER PRODUCTS: HEALY

What is Healy? Healy is a wearable, microcurrent medical device that has been cleared by the U.S. Food and Drug Administration for relief of acute, chronic, arthritis pain and muscle soreness, due to overexertion. Healy also has non-medical applications that use individualized frequencies to help balance your mind and body and relieve stress.

Why Healy and why now?

- The future of health & healing will be primarily via frequencies
- Wellness with No pills, No potions, No creams, NO hype
- Works on ALL dimensions of our health: Mental, Physical, Emotional, Spiritual, and Energetic (including Meridians and Chakras)
- Bio-energetic Field
- Digital Nutrition
- 96% effectiveness rate
- LOTS more to come, i.e. programs for stem cells, learning a new language, and even your pets, and so much more!

   As stated by Nikola Tesla,, "If you want to find the secrets of the universe, think in terms of frequency, energy and vibration." We NOW have that secret.

Healy has changed my world, my family's world and thousands of other people. I cannot imagine my life without Healy in it anymore and I'm glad I don't have to.

I truly wish for every home on the planet to have a Healy. It will rock your world.

For more info and to get an Aura Scan, head to www.kerinorley.com/healy

QUANTUM FLOW

Quantum flow is a movement practice that helps you clear your body of all the blockages that are keeping you from embodying your dreams.

As you ascend to The New Wealth, you will need to clear your field on every level to be able to hold the light that is coming through on our planet right now.

You will get to become a master of your energy and to keep a clean and pure radiance/energy field.

Quantum Flow can keep you fit and healthy as well as energetically, spiritually, mentally and emotionally clear those fields too. I mean, does it get any better?

A movement practice designed to clear the stuff keeping you from manifesting your dreams? Yes, please?!

Thank you Juan Pablo Barahona for birthing this way of life into the world. When you get into JuanPa's field, and show up for what he brings to the world, your life will never be the same again.

JuanPa is one of the most inspiring people in my life. He lives his talk and he has the biggest heart and most beautiful expression of anyone I know.

You can't help but be activated into Love when you are in his field and then choose to see and love the highest version of yourself until you become it.

JuanPa is educated and has experienced so many amazing ways of life and what he has brought together to bring to the world Quantum Flow is a gift to humanity.

Please, do yourself a favour and go to the resources page at www.kerinorley.com/resources and experience Quantum Flow.

It's just something you can't explain, you simply have to experience.

Allow Quantum Flow to help you BE in your natural state of BLISS.

It is here for you, let us show you the way.

DIGITAL CURRENCY

The 'save my butt' stuff: I AM NOT A FINANCIAL ADVISOR. What you do with any of these ways to invest is on you. I'm just giving you some resources as a place to go with people of integrity to support you in getting into the digital currency space.

What happens after this, is all on you. It's an exciting space, for sure. I highly recommend that you educate yourself so that you can invest wisely.   #sovereignty #selfresponsibility

Now that the 'save my butt' stuff is out of the way, let's play.

I have a few options for you to check out in the following pages. They are all worth looking at.

As I wrote this book, it was so important to me to bring people of integrity and that you can trust to learn from. The crypto space is a bit like the wild, wild west and there are a lot of scammy, sleazy people out there.

I personally work with both people I am sharing with you and trust them. They have been a huge part of creating Financial Sovereignty for myself.

Alright, so what next?

I invite you to consider your own risk 'profile'. Meaning, how much are you willing to risk losing? How well do you do with risk? Because that will help you make the decision on where to start in the digital currency space.

As the saying goes, don't put all your eggs in one basket. The same is true for how you invest your money. If one thing falls down and you have everything in that space, then you risk losing everything.

Diversifying your portfolio is always a good choice. Again, not a financial advisor. Speak to yours and/or start to hook into some of these tribes and get educated and make your decisions from there.

Welcome to the world of Digital Currency and the future of 'The New Wealth'.

Opportunity 1: Rossco Paddison with Decentralized Finance (DeFi)

Throughout this book, I talked about the current financial system and how that is designed for the Global Financial Elite, for control, and ultimately takes the power away from the people i.e.: you and me.

Decentralized Finance is changing the game of currency in The New Wealth. It's becoming a banking system in which you are in full, sovereign control of your money.

It really is next level financial sovereignty.

If you want to understand more about this, the easiest thing to do to dive deep into the world of Decentralized Finance is to watch this interview with Rossco Paddison. You can check it out here:

www.kerinorley.com/resources

He dives in and explains this world and how it's different to the crypto space, alone. In decentralized finance, we are still using digital currencies. How it's set up and used is where the magic is created.

THE NEW WEALTH

Depending on where in the world you live, you can get a 'debit card' that gives you access to your account and you can walk into a supermarket and spend your money. It's that easy.

Also, there is ease in getting into this system. You can be up and running in here pretty simply, which is amazing if you don't want to learn the complexities and have the risk of trading or holding crypto.

If you are interested in earning at least 7.5-8.5% compounding interest that is safe and liquid, here is an amazing opportunity for you.

If you are ready to dive in and get started with DeFi, you can join Compound Interest Alliance to learn how it works and get all the latest information about what's happening in the industry.

This is really the education platform for the deep understanding of DeFi and being able to utilize all of its intricacies.

If you are ready to get your money into the DeFi market and want to get started right away, you can go to www.kerinorley.com/resources to get started.

When you head over there, you can check out ways to be educated DeFi and ways to get started into DeFi right away.

I look forward to seeing you over there.

If you join Compound Interest Alliance you'll be hanging with Rossco, myself and many other amazing people who are also wanting to get out of the corrupt banking systems and create our own sovereignty.

Opportunity 2 - Christof Melchizedek

If you want to dive deeper into the cryptocurrency space and learn about the different coins and how to invest more into the crypto market, look no further than Christof Melchizedek.

I have never met a being who is as energetically aware and also brilliant on the real-world grounded economics and practicality of investing into the digital currency space.

Christof talks of thriving in the economic transition for the spiritually evolved.

He believes that the Blockchain and cryptocurrency provide an alternative means of exchange. From a corrupt system into one that is transparent, honest, fair, fail-safe, and free of potential tampering.

In this portal you will find the resources to help your consciousness inner-stand the power and potential of the Blockchain and how this technology will radically transform society in a way even greater than the internet.

You will also find all the resources to help get you started with making your first step into the Blockchain and crypto space. Know that the projects that he has energetically scanned are holding keys for the new infrastructure development in society 5.0. (This means investing now will make them highly explosive and profitable in the years ahead).

Getting started requires downloading some new skills and abilities, this Membership Circle aims to give you those so you can get started easily and effortlessly.

If you want more information about Christof, there is an amazing webinar that you can get access to when you go to www.kerinorley.com/resources.

I cannot recommend listening to that webinar highly enough. It's an eye-opening experience.

I have learned so much from BOTH of these men and the spaces they have created to dive into so much of the digital currency space.

Not only that, but both will speak of gold and silver investments and creating balanced portfolios.

They are both here helping all of us to create true financial sovereignty.

It has been my choice to work with both of them because they both bring different aspects to the field and I adore them both for their integrity, heart and immense knowledge in creating financial sovereignty.

People have asked me, who to invest with. I say BOTH.

Why? Because I do invest with both and will continue to because I value their experience and support so highly.

THANK YOU!

Thank you for getting this far.

Thank you for taking the time and energy to experience this book.

Thank you for allowing yourself to open to a new way of being.

I hope that whatever you do, you do not close this book and forget about it.

I truly hope that you go and check out these experiences above.

See where it feels most aligned to start your exploration of clearing your way and living in The New Wealth.

And then start.

Don't say later.

Don't say some other time.

There are free resources.

There are paid resources.

The best thing you can do for yourself right now is to go learn and experience more of this.

The time is NOW.

I look forward to connecting as we continue down this path.

It is a true honour to be walking this path with you.

THE NEW WEALTH

We are living through one of the most amazing times of evolution on this planet.

Say Yes to Sovereignty.

Say Yes to The New Wealth.

With love,
Keri

TESTIMONIALS FOR THE NEW WEALTH

Watching this book bring Keri to life has been wondrous to observe. I met Keri whilst she was in the midst of bringing together this powerful message, it brought me to Keri and many many more to come, maybe even you will get the chance to work with her in her wealth alchemy magic.

The curiosity which fuels this message will be brought into your life as you turn these pages too. I'm certain you will find new ways to relate to wealth and discover where the world is heading as this huge power shift unfolds.

Look out for the part where Keri and I talk about one of these little New Wealth Nuggets in regards to stable digital currencies that are earning outstanding interest in safe and secure ways.

Enjoy the read, but most of all enjoy your new outlook and new wealth.

Rossco Paddison

Keri is amazing with her empowering messages of The New Wealth. I read her book a couple of months back and my prosperity and wealth have improved drastically in just a few months! Thank you Keri!

Angie Kraft-Meldahl

I have had the honour of knowing Keri for over 10 years. In August 2019, I was burned-out, broke and in significant debt.

THE NEW WEALTH

I invested money that I didn't know how I was going to pay back to do The Spiral with Keri, and within 3 months I had manifested an amazing new life in Singapore and 14 months later, I'm debt-free. I cannot thank Keri enough for her energy and guidance to establish my own financial freedom.

The financial services industry is undergoing massive disruption and we need to choose a new way of managing our wealth that isn't weighted down by hidden commissions, costs and impenetrable jargon. Choosing wealth has to be conscious congruent integration of mind, body and spirit - and Keri's book shows us the way to choose sovereignty.

Justin Lodge

www.ingramcontent.com/pod-product-compliance
Lightning Source LLC
Chambersburg PA
CBHW021404210526
45463CB00001B/220